KU-610-667

Left **Communist Memorial, Wenceslas Square** Right **Modern Bohemian crystal**

Left **The Loreto** Right **St Wenceslas mural, Storch House**

PRAGUE'S
TOP 10

PRAGUE'S TOP 10

🔟 Prague's Highlights

At the geographical heart of Europe, Prague's beautiful cityscape has been carved and sustained by a variety of emperors, artists and religious communities, from the Gothic exuberance of its castle and cathedral, to the dignity of the medieval Jewish Cemetery, and the 19th-century opulence of the "new" town. Under Communist rule, Prague was off the tourist map, but since 1989 the city has seen a surge of visitors eager to take in this spectacular city.

1 Prague Castle
The hilltop fortress of the Přemyslids is home to the head of the Czech Republic. Spend a day exploring the castle's many impressive palaces, churches, galleries and gardens *(see pp8–11)*.

St Vitus's Cathedral 2
The glory of the castle complex, St Vitus's took more than 600 years to build. Visit the beautiful chapels adjoining the cathedral, or its crypt to see the tombs of Bohemia's Holy Roman Emperors *(see pp12–13)*.

3 Old Town Square
Prague's central square has been a market since the Middle Ages, and was witness to the rise and fall of numerous regimes and no shortage of bloodshed. The city has few charms finer than watching the moon rise between the towers of the Church of Our Lady Before Týn *(see pp14–17)*.

4 Charles Bridge
Linking the city across the River Vltava, it can be difficult to appreciate the beautiful carved statues of former citizens, due to the incessant crowds and trinket stalls. But it's worth the effort *(see pp18–19)*.

5 The Loreto

Pilgrims have visited this Baroque shrine to the Virgin Mary since the 17th century. Visitors can see priceless ornaments in its treasury *(see pp20–21).*

6 Old Jewish Cemetery

The jumble of tombstones in this tiny graveyard give some indication of the number of bodies buried here. Prague's Jewish community lived and worshipped in the surrounding ghetto *(see pp22–5).*

7 National Gallery

One of the first Functionalist buildings in Europe, the Trade Fair Palace now houses the National Gallery's collection of modern and contemporary art, including 14 Picassos *(see pp26–7).*

8 St Agnes's Convent

Prague's oldest Gothic building is now home to the National Gallery's collection of medieval art and remains a monument to its founder, a Přemyslid princess who gave up a life at court to pursue her faith *(see pp28–9).*

10 Petřín Hill

Perched above Malá Strana, the forested Petřín Hill is criss-crossed with footpaths, giving visitors some of the finest views in the city. The old Ukrainian church is wonderfully romantic *(see pp32–3).*

9 Wenceslas Square

From its origins as a humble horse market, Wenceslas Square has grown into a modern business centre. Monuments on the square remind visitors of its role in the nation's tumultuous history *(see pp30–31).*

🔟 Prague Castle

Crowned by the distinct spires of St Vitus's Cathedral (see pp12–13), Prague Castle (Pražský Hrad) is the metaphorical and historical throne of the Czech lands. Prince Bořivoj built a wooden fortress here in the late 9th century, establishing the hilltop overlooking the river as the Přemyslid's dynastic seat. The castle later became the capital of the Holy Roman Empire. Much of the castle was rebuilt in the 16th century, resulting in the glorious Renaissance edifice seen today. Today it is home to the President of the Czech Republic.

Main entrance

⚙ The Castle Guard changes every hour. At noon it includes a fanfare and the flag ceremony in the first courtyard.

- Hradčany, Prague 1
- Map C2 • 224 372423
- www.hrad.cz; www.praguewelcome.cz
- Castle grounds: Open Apr–Oct: 5am–midnight daily, Nov–Mar: 6am–11pm daily; Old Royal Palace, St George's Basilica, Rosenberg Palace, Golden Lane, Daliborka Tower, Prague Castle Picture Gallery and Powder Tower: Open Apr–Oct: 9am–5pm daily, Nov–Mar: 9am–4pm daily; Lobkowicz Palace, Chapel of The Holy Cross and Great South Tower: Open 10am–6pm daily
- Adm (see p9)

Top 10 Features

1. Old Royal Palace
2. South Gardens
3. Lobkowicz Palace
4. Chapel of the Holy Cross
5. St George's Convent
6. St George's Basilica
7. White Tower
8. Rosenberg Palace
9. Golden Lane
10. Daliborka Tower

Old Royal Palace
While Prince Bořivoj made do with a wooden structure, subsequent residences were built on top of each other as the tastes of Bohemia's rulers changed *(see pp10–11)*. Halls are decorated with coats of arms *(above)*.

South Gardens
Ferdinand I and his son Maximilian II gave the dour castle some greenery in the late 16th century, and the First Republic architect Josip Plečnik created the lined paths, steps and grottoes *(right)* that extend to Malá Strana.

Lobkowicz Palace
Opened by the Lobkowicz family in 2007, this rival to the National Gallery holds works by Bruegel, Canaletto, Dürer, Rubens and Velázquez in its unique collection.

4 Chapel of the Holy Cross

Built by the Italian architect Anselmo Lurago in 1763, this chapel houses the Treasure of St Vitus exhibition.

5 St George's Convent

Prince Boleslav II with Princess Mlada established the first Czech convent here in the 10th century. The Romanesque building is not open to the public.

Plan of Prague Castle

9 Golden Lane

The colourful hovels *(below)* built into the castle wall were home to goldsmiths so they could avoid guild dues in town.

10 Daliborka Tower

Dalibor, something of a Czech Robin Hood, was captured and became the first prisoner of the tower that now takes his name *(below)*.

6 St George's Basilica

Prince Vratislav built the basilica in AD 921. The chapel of St Wenceslas's grandmother, St Ludmila, is decorated with beautiful 16th-century paintings *(below)*.

7 White Tower

The White Tower contains a torture chamber and, today, shops selling grisly souvenirs. The gangways from which archers once watched over the moat are lined with replicas of weapons.

8 Rosenberg Palace

This 16th-century palace has had multiple uses during its history: as a residence for noblewomen, as part of the Ministry of Internal Affairs of Czechoslovakia and as presidential offices.

Castle Guide

You can wander through much of the castle complex for free, but to see the interiors, buy a ticket at the office in the third courtyard. A Kč250 ticket includes entry to St George's Basilica, the Old Royal Palace, Golden Lane, Daliborka Tower and St Vitus's Cathedral; a Kč350 ticket also includes entry to Rosenberg Palace and the Powder Tower.

Left **Bohemian Chancellery** Right **Vault in the old Land Rolls Room**

🔟 Features of the Royal Palace

1 Vladislav Hall
Benedict Ried created a mastery of Gothic design with his elaborate vaulting here. Since the First Republic, the country's presidents have been ceremoniously chosen here, but it has also been used for coronations and jousting tournaments.

2 Riders' Staircase
The low steps and vaulted ceiling of this stairway permitted mounted knights to make spectacular entrances to tournaments held in Vladislav Hall.

3 Louis Wing
Only 10 years and a few steps separate the southern wing from the main hall, but in the interim, Benedict Ried moved castle architecture from Gothic to Renaissance. Bohemian nobles met here in an administrative body when the king was away.

The Diet

4 Bohemian Chancellery
The first battle of the Thirty Years' War was staged here. Protestant noblemen threw two Catholic governors and their secretary from the east window. Their fall was broken by a dung heap – or an intervening angel, depending on who you ask.

5 Old Land Rolls Room
The coats of arms decorating the walls belong to clerks who kept tabs on property ownership and court decisions from 1614 to 1777. Until the reign of Maria Theresa, record books were not numbered, but identified by elaborate covers.

6 Diet
Bohemian nobles met here with the king in a prototype parliament. The king sat on the throne (the one seen today is a 19th-century replica), the archbishop sat to the king's right, while the estates sat on his left. The portraits on the wall show, from the left, Maria Theresa, her husband Franz, Josef II, Leopold II and Franz I, who fought Napoleon at Austerlitz.

Riders' Staircase

Discover more at **www.traveldk.com**

7 Chapel of All Saints

At the eastern end of Vladislav Hall, a doorway leads to a balcony above the Chapel of All Saints. Peter Parléř's modelled it on the Gothic Sainte-Chapelle in Paris. After fire destroyed it in 1541, it was redesigned in Renaissance style. Of particular artistic note is Hans van Aachen's *Triptych of the Angels*.

8 Soběslav Residence

Prince Soběslav literally laid the foundations for Prague Castle, building the first stone palace here in the 12th century.

9 The Story of Prague Castle

This permanent exhibition covers the history, events, personalities and arts and crafts relating to the main castle complex, making for an informative and entertaining experience.

10 Busts from Peter Parléř's Workshop

These impressive portraits were created in the late 14th century and include the grandfather-father-grandson set of John of Luxembourg, Charles IV and Wenceslas IV.

Prague's Top 10

Top 10 Rulers of Prague

1. Wenceslas (around 907–935)
2. Otakar II (1233–78)
3. Charles IV (1316–78)
4. Wenceslas IV (1361–1419)
5. Rudolph II (1552–1612)
6. Tomáš Garrigue Masaryk (1850–1937)
7. Edvard Beneš (1884–1948)
8. Klement Gottwald (1896–1953)
9. Václav Havel (b.1936)
10. Václav Klaus (b.1941)

Prague's Third Defenestration

Prague's first recorded instance of execution by hurling the condemned from a window occurred at the outset of the Hussite Wars in 1419. Vladislav II's officials met a similar fate in 1483. Perhaps as a tribute to their forebears, more than 100 Protestant nobles stormed the Old Royal Palace in 1618 and cast two hated Catholic governors and their secretary out of the window. The men's fall was broken by a dung heap swept from the Vladislav Hall after a recent tournament (although Catholics at the time claim they were saved by angels). The incident is often cited as the spark that began the Thirty Years' War. Following the Protestants' defeat at Bílá Hora in 1620, the nobles got their day in court and at the gallows, in front of the Old Town Hall (see pp16–17).

Prague's Defenestration
This 1889 work by Václav von Brožík captures the moment of the Protestants' attack on the Catholic governors. Painted 271 years later, it illustrates how the event has remained in the Czech consciousness.

St Vitus's Cathedral

This spectacular Gothic cathedral is an unmissable sight in Prague, not least because of its dominant position on Hradčany hill, looming over the Vltava and the rest of the city. Prince Wenceslas first built a rotunda here on a pagan worship site and dedicated it to St Vitus (svatý Vít), a Roman saint. Matthew d'Arras began work on the grand cathedral in 1344 when Prague was named an archbishopric. He died shortly thereafter and Charles IV hired the Swabian wunderkind Peter Parléř to take over. With the intervention of the Hussite Wars, however, work stopped and, remarkably, construction was only finally completed in 1929.

Great Tower windows

The western half of St Vitus's Cathedral can be appreciated for free. An admission fee is charged for other areas.

Seeing all that the cathedral and the castle have to offer can take a whole day. The Royal Crypt may be entered with a guide.

• Third Courtyard, Prague Castle
• Map C2
• 224 371111
• www.hrad.cz
• Open Mar–Oct: 9am–5pm Mon–Sat, noon–5pm Sun; Nov–Feb: 9am–4pm Mon–Sat, noon–4pm Sun; South Tower: 10am–7pm daily (to 5pm Nov–Mar)
• Adm Kč250 or Kč350 (see p9)

Top 10 Features

1. South Tower
2. Wenceslas Chapel
3. Bohemian Crown Jewels
4. Royal Crypt
5. Royal Oratory
6. St John of Nepomuk's Tomb
7. New Archbishop's Chapel
8. Sigismund
9. Golden Portal
10. High Altar

South Tower

It is clear at exactly which point the Hussite civil wars halted construction of this 96-m (315-ft) tower. By the time work resumed, architectural style had moved into the Renaissance, hence the rounded cap on a Gothic base. The tower is closed to the public.

Wenceslas Chapel

This chapel *(left)* stands where Prince Wenceslas built the first St Vitus rotunda and contains the tomb of its namesake, Bohemia's patron saint. The frescoes of Christ's Passion on the lower wall are surrounded by 1,300 semi-precious stones. Vladislav II commissioned the upper frescoes of St Wenceslas's life, painted to celebrate his son Ludvik's coronation.

For more places of worship in Prague See pp38–9

Bohemian Crown Jewels

You'd think there would be a safer place for the crown and sceptre of Bohemia, but the coronation chamber of Wenceslas Chapel is said to be guarded by the spirit of the saint.

St John of Nepomuk's Tomb

The silver for this 1,680-kg (3,700-lb) coffin *(above)* came from the Bohemian mining town of Kutná Hora, symbolized by the statues of miners to the left of the tomb.

New Archbishop's Chapel

Alfons Mucha created the Art Nouveau window of the Slavic saints for the Archbishop's Chapel *(below)*. Despite appearances, the glass is painted, not stained.

Sigismund

The 18-tonne bell of the Great Tower *(below)*, affectionately known as Sigismund, is the nation's largest and dates from 1549. It takes four volunteers to ring the bell on important church holidays and events.

Royal Crypt

The greatest kings of Bohemia are buried in a single room beneath the cathedral, including Charles IV, Wenceslas IV and Rudolf II.

Royal Oratory

The royal family crossed a narrow bridge from the Royal Palace *(see p8)* to this private gallery to hear mass. The coats of arms represent all the countries that were ruled by Vladislav II.

Cathedral Floorplan

Golden Portal

This triple-arched arcade *(above)* was the main entrance to the cathedral until the western end was completed in the 20th century.

High Altar

Bounded by St Vitus's Chapel and the marble sarcophagi of Ferdinand I and family, the high altar and chancel *(centre)* follow a strict Neo-Gothic philosophy.

Peter Parléř

After the death of Matthew d'Arras, Charles IV made Parléř his chief architect. Parléř undertook St Vitus's Cathedral, Charles Bridge and numerous other Gothic monuments that still stand in Prague. He trained many artisans, and his talented sons and nephews continued his work after his death in 1399.

Prague's Top 10

13

⁵⁵10 Old Town Square

As the heart and soul of the city, no visitor should, or is likely to miss the Old Town Square (Staroměstské náměstí). A marketplace was located here in the 11th century, but it was in 1338, when John of Luxembourg gave Prague's burghers permission to form a town council, that the Old Town Hall was built (see p16) and the square came into its own. Today, it has a lively atmosphere, with café tables set out in front of painted façades, horses and carts waiting to ferry tourists around the city and street-sellers hawking their wares.

Jan Hus Memorial

✪ Resist the temptation to climb on the Jan Hus Monument. Doing so, or trampling the flowers, will earn you a fine, as well as embarrassment.

- Map M3
- Old Town Hall: Staroměstské náměstí 1, 236 002629;
Open 11am–6pm Mon, 9am–6pm Tue–Sun;
Tower: 11am–10pm Mon, 9am–10pm Tue–Sun;
Sewer (Cellars): 10am–10pm daily
- Adm Kč100 for hall and cellars; Adm Kč110 for tower

Top 10 Features

1. Dům u Minuty
2. House at the Stone Bell
3. Church of Our Lady Before Týn
4. Church of St Nicholas
5. Jan Hus Memorial
6. Marian Column
7. Ungelt
8. Štorch House
9. Golz-Kinský Palace
10. Malé náměstí

1 Dům u Minuty
The "House at the Minutes" *(above)* probably takes its name from the not-so-minute *sgraffito* images on its walls. The alchemical symbols adorning Staroměstské náměstí 2 date from 1611. Franz Kafka lived in the black-and-white house as a boy *(see p44)*.

2 House at the Stone Bell
Formerly done up in Baroque style, workers discovered the Gothic façade of this house as late as 1980. On the southwestern corner is the bell which gives the house its name. The Municipal Gallery often hosts temporary exhibitions here.

3 Church of Our Lady Before Týn
This Gothic edifice *(below)* began as a humble church serving residents in the mercantile town *(týn)* in the 14th century. Following architectural customs of the time, the south tower is stouter than the north one *(see p38)*.

Church of St Nicholas
Prague has two Baroque churches of St Nicholas, both built by Kilian Ignac Dientzenhoffer. The architect completed the one in Old Town *(right)* two years before starting Malá Strana's *(see p82)*. Regular concerts here give visitors a chance to hear the church's organ.

Malé náměstí
The ornate well in the centre of the "Small Square" doubles as a plague memorial. The elaborate murals of craftsmen on the façade of Rott House *(below)* are the only decoration now left. Until the early 1990s, the building was a hardware shop.

Jan Hus Memorial
Hus was burned at the stake in 1415 for proposing radical Church reform. The inscription below the figure of Hus reads "Truth Will Prevail".

Marian Column
On Czechoslovakia's declaration of independence in 1918, this former column reminded jubilant mobs of Habsburg rule and they tore it down. A plan is afoot to rebuild it.

Ungelt
The courtyard behind Týn church was home to foreign merchants in the 14th century, but today it is home to smart boutiques and cafés.

Štorch House
An Art Nouveau equestrian painting of St Wenceslas is the focal point of the house at Staroměstské náměstí 16.

Golz-Kinský Palace
Once occupied by Communists, this former palace *(centre & below)* now houses the National Gallery's collection of prints and drawings and an up-market restaurant.

Jan Hus

The rector of Prague (later Charles) University, Jan Hus was dedicated to fighting against corruption in the Church. He was declared a heretic by the Church, and was summoned to Germany where he was burned at the stake. Czech resentment turned into civil war, with Hussite rebels facing the power of Rome. But the Hussites split into moderate and radical factions, the former defeating the latter in 1434. Hus is still a national figure – 6th July, the day he was killed, is a public holiday.

Left **Apostles** Centre **Crosses, White Mountain Memorial** Right **Gothic Chapel**

Old Town Hall Features

Astronomical Clock
During the day, on the hour, bells ring, cocks crow and 15th-century statues dance while crowds of tourists watch from below.

Apostles
Marionette artist Vojtěch Sucharda sculpted the 12 wooden figures that turn out for the crowds on the astronomical clock – they replace the ones destroyed by German artillery in 1945. A brochure identifies which saint is which.

Art Gallery
On the Old Town Hall's ground floor is an exhibition space which features temporary shows.

Dukla Memorial
Behind a brass plaque identified by the year "1945" is a pot of soil from the Dukla battle-field. German artillery gunned down 84,000 Red Army soldiers in this Slovak pass in one of the most grievous military miscalculations of World War II.

White Mountain Memorial
Twenty-seven crosses are set in the pavement on the town hall's eastern side in memory of the Bohemian nobles who were executed for their role in the Thirty Years' War *(see p34)*. After Protestant forces were defeated at the Battle of White Mountain, the men were hanged, beheaded or drawn and quartered here in a public ceremony.

Gothic Chapel
The small chapel adjoining the Mayors' Hall was consecrated in 1381 in honour of the saints Wenceslas, Vitus and Ludmila. Wenceslas IV's emblem and his wife Eufemia's initial adorn the entrance portal. In the nave is a scale model of the Marian column which stood on the Old Town Square until 1918 and may be rebuilt *(see p15)*.

Elevator
The elevator taking visitors up to the viewing gallery of the tower won an award for best design in 1999. Oddly enough, its space-age design works harmoniously within the stony surroundings. It also permits wheelchair access to the top of the tower – a rare consideration in Prague.

Church of St Nicholas seen from the Viewing Gallery

While you're enjoying the hourly astronomical clock performance, keep an eye on your wallet as well as the show.

Viewing Gallery

8 The parapet under the Old Town Hall's roof affords visitors a unique view of the square and the Old Town below. Bring your pocket change: Kč20 will buy you two minutes on a miniature telescope, with which you can admire the entire Prague Valley.

Craft stalls lining The Green

Gothic Cellars

9 The cellars of the Old Town Hall were once ground floor rooms. The town was subject to flooding, so more earth was added to keep burghers' feet dry. The spaces were used as granaries and debtors' prisons.

The Green

10 Retreating German artillery unloaded their guns on the Old Town Hall's north wing to avoid carrying the shells back to Berlin. After the war, the wing was torn down. Now the area is lined with stalls selling Czech handicrafts.

Top 10 Features of the Astronomical Clock

1. Solar clock
2. Lunar clock
3. Josef Mánes Calendar
4. Apostles
5. Angel and the Sciences
6. Vanity, Avarice, Death and Lust
7. Rooster
8. Hourly Shows
9. Master Hanuš
10. Dial

Building the Old Town Hall

Prague's Old Town received its charter and fortifications from John of Luxembourg in the mid-13th century, but its town clerk had to wait nearly 150 years for an office. The Old Town Hall was cobbled together from existing houses over the centuries until it comprised the five houses that stand at Staroměstské náměstí 1–2 today. The hall's eastern wing once stretched to within a few feet of the door of the Church of St Nicholas (see p15), but German artillery reduced it to rubble in 1945. The clock tower was installed in 1410, but the clock wasn't up and running until 1572.

Medieval Astrology

The Astronomical Clock's face not only tells the time, but also relates the movement of the planets around earth, and the sun and moon through the signs of the zodiac. It is decorated with paintings by Josef Mánes.

Charles Bridge

The spectacular Charles Bridge (Karlův most) has witnessed processions, battles, executions and, increasingly, film shoots since its construction between 1357 and 1402. Peter Parléř (see p13) built the viaduct to replace its predecessor, the Judith Bridge, in Gothic style. The bridge's most distinguishing feature is its gallery of 30 statues. The saints and other religious figures were installed, from 1683 onwards, to lead the people back to mass. Some, such as Braun's St Luitgard, are incomparably lovely; others, such as Bohn's Calvary, are politically controversial. Today all the statues are reproductions – the originals are preserved in museums across the city.

Old Town Bridge Tower detail

🔘 **The Malá Strana Bridge Tower houses an exhibit on the bridge's history.**

• Map J4
• Malá Strana Bridge Tower: 607 050434; Open Apr–Sep: 10am–10pm; Nov–Feb: 10am–6pm; Mar & Oct: 10am–8pm; Adm Kč90
• Old Town Bridge Tower: Exhibition about the bridge and Charles IV and his life: 224 220569; Open Apr–Sep: 10am–10pm; Nov–Feb: 10am–6pm; Mar & Oct: 10am–8pm; Adm Kč90

Top 10 Features

1. Old Town Bridge Tower
2. Calvary
3. The Lorraine Cross
4. Statue of St John of Nepomuk
5. Statue of Sts Cyril and Methodius
6. Statue of Bruncvik
7. Our Lady of the Mangles
8. Statue of St Luitgard
9. Antonin
10. Statue of the Trinitarian Order

Old Town Bridge Tower

From the parapet of the Old Town bridge tower, you can see the gentle S-curve that the architect Peter Parléř built into the viaduct to obstruct invaders, as well as a jaw-dropping panorama of the city.

Calvary

This statue *(right)* will cause double-takes among students of Hebrew. According to a nearby apologia, the words "Holy, holy, holy is the Lord of Hosts" were added in 1696, paid for by a local Jewish man who had been accused of profaning the cross.

The Lorraine Cross

Halfway across the bridge is a brass cross where John Nepomuk's body was thrown into the river *(see p35)*. It is said that if you wish on the cross the wish will come true.

4 Statue of St John of Nepomuk

Rubbing the brass relief *(right)* of the saint shown diving into the river is an old tradition, thought to bring good luck; petting the adjacent brass dog is a new one.

6 Statue of Bruncvik

Peer over the bridge's southern edge to see the Czech's answer to King Arthur. Bruncvik and his army are promised to awaken and save Prague at the city's most desperate hour.

7 Our Lady of the Mangles

The portrait of Mary hanging on the house south of the bridge *(above)* is tied to an ancient tale of miraculous healing. Seeing the light go out on the balcony below is supposedly an omen of imminent death – don't stare too long.

Statue of Sts Cyril & Methodius 5

Greek missionaries who brought both Christianity and the Cyrillic alphabet to the Czech and Slovak lands, Cyril and Methodius are national heroes of both countries to this day. Karel Dvořák created this statue *(right)* in 1928–1938 at the peak of Czechoslovakia's period of National Awakening, following independence.

8 Statue of St Luitgard

Matthias Brauns' 1710 depiction of a blind nun's dream, in which the crucified Christ permitted her to touch his wounds *(below)*, retains a timeless appeal.

9 Antonín

One of many artists selling work from the bridge, Antonín paints portraits of himself as the devil. His proximity to the Čertovka (Devil's Canal) may be the key.

10 Statue of the Trinitarian Order

This religious order was set up to ransom prisoners of war from the Crusades and buy Chris-tians back their freedom; hence the bored Turk guarding the cell.

When to Visit Charles Bridge

During summer, and increasingly year-round, the bridge is well nigh impassable throughout the day, crowded with artists, tourists and the odd Dixieland jazz band. It's best seen in the early hours as the sun rises over the Old Town bridge tower. A late evening stroll gives a similarly dramatic view, with the illuminated St Nicholas's Church and castle looming above.

The Loreto

At the heart of this sparkling 17th-century Baroque pilgrimage site is its claim to fame and most proud possession: a replica of the original Santa Casa in Loreto, Italy, believed to be the house where the Virgin Mary received the Incarnation. Construction of the grandiose church and the surrounding chapels coincided with the Counter Reformation, and one of Prague's first Baroque buildings was intended to lure Czechs back to the Catholic faith.

Loreto entrance

Top 10 Features
1. Loretánské náměstí
2. Santa Casa
3. Bell Tower
4. Inner Courtyard
5. Arcade
6. St Wilgifortis Altar
7. Church of the Nativity
8. Altars of Sts Felicissimus and Marcia
9. Treasury
10. Diamond Monstrance

🕐 Just around the corner from the Loreto, at Kapucínská 2, is a monument to people tortured by the secret police at the former Interior Ministry building.

- Loretánské náměstí 7
- Map A2
- 220 516740
- www.loreta.cz
- Open 9am–12:15pm & 1–4:30pm Tue–Sun
- Adm Kč130

1 Loretánské náměstí
This square is said to have been a pagan burial ground. The stucco façade of the Loreto *(above)* is dwarfed by the Černín Palace opposite, home of the Ministry of Foreign Affairs.

2 Santa Casa
The stucco reliefs on the outside of this replica of the Holy Family's house in Nazareth depict scenes from the Virgin Mary's life. Inside is the miracle-working statue of Our Lady of Loreto.

3 Bell Tower
The carillon *(below)* was the gift of a Prague merchant whose daughter was healed by the intercession of the Lady of Loreto. An automated mechanism chimes a Marian hymn every hour.

Plan of The Loreto

4 Inner Courtyard

In the inner courtyard, visitors can admire two Baroque fountains. The north fountain features a sculpture of the Resurrection; the south, the Assumption of the Virgin Mary *(right)*.

9 Treasury

The Communists crafted this exhibit of sacred gold and silver items to show how peasants were brought to obedience with this "cheap promise of happiness beyond the grave".

10 Diamond Monstrance

The silver work by Johann Bernard Fischer von Erlach is covered with 6,222 diamonds. The Virgin looks up at her son, represented by the host in the receptacle.

5 Arcade

Before and after visiting the Santa Casa, pilgrims passed through the arcade and prayed at its chapels of St Anne, St Francis Seraphim, the Holy Family, the Holy Rood, St Antony of Padua and Our Lady of Sorrows.

6 St Wilgifortis Altar

The Chapel of Our Lady of Sorrows is dominated by the sight of a crucified, bearded woman. St Wilgifortis was a Portuguese maiden who prayed for a masculine appearance to preserve her chastity.

7 Church of the Nativity

Originally a small alcove behind the Santa Casa, the church was expanded into its present size in 1717. The Rococo organ stands opposite the altar, over a crypt to Loreto benefactors.

8 Altars of Sts Felicissimus and Marcia

On either side of the altar in the Church of the Nativity are large reliquary displays containing the remains of these two Spanish saints.

Santa Casa

The Santa Casa was the Nazareth house in which the archangel Gabriel is believed to have announced to the Virgin Mary that she would conceive the Son of God. In the 13th century, the Greek Angeli family moved the house to Loreto, Italy. As the Marian cult spread, copies of the Loreto started emerging all over Europe – the Prague site *(below)* is believed to be the truest representation of the original.

Old Jewish Cemetery

The crumbling image of the Old Jewish Cemetery is a moving memorial to Prague's once considerable Jewish community. As this was one of few burial sites available to Prague's Jews, when the plot was full, graves were built up in layers – estimates put the number at about 200,000, with the oldest headstone dating from 1439. The final burial took place in 1787, but stroll through the enclosure and you'll get a sense of noble lives once lived.

Rabbi Loew's Grave

⭐ It is customary for men to wear a *yarmulka* (skull cap) in the synagogues. Look for them near the entrance, but return it when you leave.

The Museum of Decorative Arts' east-facing windows offer an excellent crowd-free view of the cemetery *(see p37).*

• Old Jewish Cemetery: U Starého hřbitova 3, Map K3, 224 819456, www.jewishmuseum.cz, Open Apr–Oct: 9am–6pm Sun–Fri; Nov–Mar: 9am–4:30pm; Closed Jewish holidays, Adm Kč300 (ticket valid for 1 week, includes entrance to various synagogues; euros accepted)
• Old-New Synagogue: Pařížská, Map K3, Open 9:30am–6pm Sun–Fri (to 5pm Nov–Mar), Adm Kč200

Top 10 Features

1. Avigdor Kara's Grave
2. Mordecai Maisel's Grave
3. Rabbi Loew's Grave
4. David Gans's Tombstone
5. Klausen Synagogue
6. Rabbi Oppenheim's Grave
7. Gothic Tombstones
8. Hendl Bashevi's Grave
9. Zemach Graves
10. Nephele Mound

1 Avigdor Kara's Grave
The oldest grave is that of this poet and scholar, best known for his documentation of the pogrom of 1389, which he survived.

2 Mordecai Maisel's Grave
Mordecai Maisel (1528–1601) was ghetto mayor during the reign of Rudolf II, and funded the synagogue that bears his name *(see p100).*

3 Rabbi Loew's Grave
The burial site of one of Prague's major Jewish figures, Rabbi Jehuda Loew ben Bezalel (1520–1609), and creator of the Golem *(see p52).*

4 David Gans's Tombstone
A pupil of Rabbi Loew, Gans (1541–1613) was the author of a seminal two-volume history of the Jewish people. He was also an accomplished astronomer during the time of Johannes Kepler *(see p35).* His headstone *(right)* is marked with the Star of David, after his name and his faith.

5 Klausen Synagogue
Mordecai Maisel also commissioned the building of the Klausen Synagogue *(left)* on the cemetery's northern edge. It now houses exhibitions on Jewish festivals and traditions.

Rabbi Oppenheim's Grave

Rabbi David Oppenheim (*left*) was the first chief rabbi of Moravia, and later chief rabbi of Bohemia and finally of Prague, where he died in 1736.

Plan of the Old Jewish Cemetery

Zemach Graves

Next to the Pinkas Synagogue (*see p101*) is a square gravestone where Mordechai Zemach (d. 1592) is buried with his son Bezalel (d. 1589). The name Zemach means "spring" in Hebrew.

Nephele Mound

Stillborn children, miscarried babies and other infants who died under a year old were buried in the southeast corner of the cemetery.

Hendl Bashevi's Grave

This elaborate tombstone (*below*) marks the resting place of the so-called "Jewish Queen", Hendl Bashevi. Her husband, mayor Jacob Bashevi, was knighted and permitted a coat of arms, seen on his wife's gravestone.

Gothic Tombstones

The eastern wall of the cemetery holds fragments of Gothic tombstones (*above*) rescued in 1866 from another graveyard near Vladislavova street. Further graves at another site were uncovered in the 1990s.

Grave Symbols

As a rule, a Hebrew tombstone (*matzevah*) contains the deceased's name, date of death and eulogy. In addition to these basics, the grave-markers in the Old Jewish Cemetery often included symbolic images indicating the deceased's lineage. Names are often symbolized by animals, according to Biblical precedent or Hebrew or Germanic translations – David Gans's tombstone features a goose (*gans* in German). Some professions are also represented: scissors may appear on a tailor's tombstone, for example.

Left **Façade** Centre **Vaulting** Right **Nave**

Features in the Old-New Synagogue

1 Rabbi Loew's Chair
Topped with a Star of David, the tall chair found by the eastern wall has been reserved for Prague's chief rabbis throughout the synagogue's history.

2 Jewish Standard
Prague's Jewish community was permitted a banner in the 15th century as a symbol of its autonomy. The copy hanging above the Bimah replicates a 1716 original, featuring a Jewish hat within a six-pointed star and the legend *"Shema Yisroel".*

3 Nave
Twelve narrow windows, evoking the 12 tribes of Israel, line the perimeter walls, which are unadorned, save for the abbreviation of Biblical verses. Two central pillars are modelled on the façade columns of the Temple of Jerusalem.

4 Ark
Behind the curtain on the eastern wall are the Torah scrolls, which are kept in the holy ark. The tympanum features foliage and grape motifs, also found in nearby St Agnes's Convent *(see pp28–9)*, and date from the synagogue's construction in the late 13th century.

Rabbi Loew's Chair

5 Entrance
The biblical inscription "Revere God and observe His commandments! For this applies to all mankind" admonished worshippers entering and leaving the synagogue.

6 Vaulting
To avoid the sign of the cross, a fifth rib was added to the nave's vaulting, decorated with vine leaves and ivy.

7 Women's Windows
Women were not permitted in the nave of the synagogue, but sat in the vestibule. Narrow openings in the wall allowed them to follow the services.

8 Bimah
A pulpit stands on this dais in the centre. From here the rabbi reads the Torah and performs wedding ceremonies.

9 Attic
Legend has it that Rabbi Loew stashed the remains of the Golem *(see p52)* under the synagogue's large saddle roof.

10 Josefov Town Hall
Adjacent to the synagogue is the Jewish Town Hall. The façade clock's hands run counter-clockwise – or clockwise, if you read Hebrew *(see p99).*

For more Places of Worship **See pp38–9**

Top 10 Jewish Leaders

1. Eliezer ben Elijah Ashkenazi (1512–85)
2. Judah Loew ben Bezalel (1520–1609)
3. Mordecai Maisel (1528–1601)
4. Mordecai ben Abraham Jaffe (1530–1612)
5. Ephraim Solomon ben Aaron of Luntshits (1550–1619)
6. Joseph Solomon Delmedigo (1591–1655)
7. David ben Abraham Oppenheim (1664–1736)
8. Yechezkel ben Yehuda Landau (1713–93)
9. Solomon Judah Lieb Rapoport (1790–1867)
10. Efraim Karol Sidon (b. 1942)

Prague Ghetto
During World War II, Prague's Jews were moved to a town called Terezín, later the site of a concentration camp.

The Jews in Prague

Prague's Jews have been plagued by anti-Semitic behaviour almost since their arrival in the 10th century. Zealous Christians destroyed an early settlement in what is now Malá Strana. Such pogroms were not uncommon – the most infamous is the Passover slaughter of 1389, in which rioters killed more than 3,000 Jews, including those who had taken refuge in the Old-New Synagogue. But there were high points. Prominent Jews – notably Rabbi Loew and Mordecai Maisel – enjoyed influence in Rudolf II's court; Charles VI recognized the community's autonomy in 1716; his descendant Joseph II ended many discriminatory measures; and, in the late 19th century, Jews were active in the National Revival. But anti-Semitism still lurked. In 1899, Leopold Hilsner was accused of ritual murder; his counsel was Tomáš Garrigue Masaryk, future president of independent Czechoslovakia. Although the interwar years were a golden age for Czech Jews, among them Franz Kafka (see p44), the 1938 Munich Agreement gave Hitler possession of Czech lands, and the Jews' freedom was restricted to a ghetto, before being deported to concentration camps. Synagogues were turned into archives for looted Jewish artifacts. Hitler reportedly even planned to create a museum of an extinct race in Josefov. By the end of the war nearly 80,000 Bohemian and Moravian Jews had died in the Holocaust.

Father and son moving their belongings to the "ghetto" of Terezín

National Gallery

Surrounded by the decorative Art Nouveau buildings of Holešovice, the austere Trade Fair Palace is a daring work of art in itself. It was the first official Functionalist building in Europe, and even Le Corbusier was impressed by the eight-storey edifice when he visited Prague in 1928. After years as a trade fair complex, plans to turn the building into the home of the National Gallery's modern art collection were launched in 1979. Alongside prominent Czech contributions to modern art is a rich array of international masters from the 19th, 20th and 21st centuries.

Trade Fair Palace façade

● The café on the ground floor also doubles as an Internet café.

✪ The first floor houses short-term exhibits. Check the weekly galleries listings of the *Prague Post* for details *(see p128)*. The exhibits shown on these pages are on the third floor.

Dukelských hrdinu 47, Holešovice
• Map B5
• 224 301122
• www.ngprague.cz
• Open 10am–6pm Tue–Sun
• Dis. access
• Adm Kč200

Top 10 Paintings

1. House in Aix-en-Provence
2. Bonjour, Monsieur Gauguin
3. Rider Jaguar Attacking a Horseman
4. Green Wheat
5. St John the Baptist
6. Head of a Young Girl
7. At the Moulin Rouge
8. Myself, Self Portrait
9. Self Portrait
10. Anxiety

Entrance

House in Aix-en-Provence
The National Gallery's impressive collection of French art was begun in 1923, when Czech president Tomáš Masaryk helped found a small collection. This bright landscape *(above)* by Paul Cézanne was one of those original 25 pieces.

Bonjour, Monsieur Gauguin
Paul Gauguin's simple, flat self-portrait *(right)* was originally painted as a decoration for the lower panel of a dining-room door for a house in Brittany. The much-admired 19th-century French artist made this enlarged copy in 1889.

For details of other National Gallery sites in Prague See p36

3 Rider Jaguar Attacking a Horseman

Delacroix often visited zoos to study predatory animals whose movement inspired him. This small canvas from 1853 *(right)* is a fine example of such research, and is striking for its interaction of colour and motion.

5 St John the Baptist

Auguste Rodin's 1878 sculpture *(below)* is a study of spiral motion, from the tension of the firmly anchored feet, to the rotating trunk, to the head turned away from the dominant gesture of the right hand.

8 Myself, Self Portrait

With elements of modern civilization in the background, Henri Rousseau's self-portrait depicts the artist as a self-assured personality.

9 Self-Portrait

One of 14 Picassos donated by former National Museum director Vincenc Kramář in 1960, the almond-shaped eyes and triangular nose testify to the influence of Iberian art and sculpture.

10 Anxiety

Otto Gutfreund paved the way for modern Czech sculpture. This bronze *(above)* captures the apprehension of man in the early 20th century.

4 Green Wheat

Van Gogh's encounter with Impressionism was a decisive moment. Charmed by the countryside of southern France, he began to create bright canvases such as this landscape *(below)*.

6 Head of a Young Girl

Created in 1926, Henri Laurens' sculpture is a synthesis of Cubism and the Classical ideal of form and beauty. The National Gallery added Laurens' bronze to its collection in 1935.

7 At the Moulin Rouge

Toulouse-Lautrec thrived on depictions of Paris nightlife such as this oil tempera on cardboard. One of the dancing women is his muse, Jane Avril. Oscar Wilde is one of the figures in the background.

Functionalism

Plans for a trade fair complex began in 1924. A design competition selected the work of architects Oldřich Týl and Josef Fuchs. Only the existing Trade Fair Palace was completed; other planned buildings never materialized due to a lack of funding. The Trade Fair Palace opened in 1928 on the Republic's 10th anniversary. It was badly damaged by fire in 1974 and reopened to the public in 1995.

ᴛᴏᴘ 10 St Agnes's Convent

The 13th-century Convent of St Agnes of Bohemia (Klášter sv. Anežky) is an impressive Gothic building, closely tied to Czech statehood. Daughter of Přemysl Otakar I, Princess Agnes chose a spiritual life and founded a convent here in 1234 for the Poor Clares, an order of nuns associated with the Order of St Francis. But it was Agnes's diplomatic skills and work in establishing the convent which raised Bohemia in the eyes of Rome, as much as any courtly efforts to do the same. Restored in the 1980s to its original splendour, the convent is now used by the National Gallery to exhibit its collection of medieval and early Renaissance art.

Convent façade

⊘ With the exception of short-term exhibitions, the ground floor of the convent building is empty, but frequent chamber music concerts give visitors the opportunity to appreciate the pure Gothic spaces.

- U Milosrdných 17
- Map M1
- 224 810628
- www.ngprague.cz
- Open 10am–6pm Tue–Sun
- Dis. access
- Adm Kč150

Top 10 Works of Art

1. Strakonice Madonna
2. Zbraslav Madonna
3. Vyšší Brod Altarpiece
4. Works of Master Theodoricus
5. Třeboň Altarpiece
6. Capuchin Cycle
7. Velhartice Altarpiece
8. Martyrdom of St Florian
9. Puchner Altarpiece
10. Apocalypse Cycle

1 Strakonice Madonna

This larger-than-life, 700-year-old statue *(below)* of the Virgin and Child is the Czech National Gallery's most prized possession. The gestures of the Madonna are strikingly rigid, and evoke the Classical French sculpture found in places such as Reims Cathedral.

2 Zbraslav Madonna

Bohemia's most celebrated Marian painting is evocative of Byzantine icons in its style. The ring on the Madonna's left-hand finger symbolizes the Church through the mystical marriage between Christ and the Virgin Mary. The work has been moved to St Agnes's Convent from a Cistercian monastery where the majority of the Přemyslid kings were laid to rest.

3 Vyšší Brod Altarpiece

The 14th-century cycle begins with the *Annunciation*, then proceeds through the *Adoration of the Magi (below)* to *Pentecost (right)*. The creator of these beautiful panels is unknown.

Floorplan of St Agnes' Convent

Entrance

6 Capuchin Cycle

The origin of these 14 panels is unknown. The Virgin Mary is flanked by St Peter on the left and Christ on the right.

9 Puchner Altarpiece

St Agnes gave up a life at court to pursue a spiritual vocation. She is typically depicted nursing the sick on this 15th-century altarpiece.

10 Apocalypse Cycle

Although he's considered the foremost German Renaissance artist, Albrecht Dürer is probably best known for woodcuts such as this series of 15 from 1498 *(below)*, which retain a strong Gothic flavour.

7 Velhartice Altarpiece

Originating in south Bohemia around 1500, this is a rare example of a completely preserved altar *(above)*. Beneath the Madonna, cherubs hold the vera icon.

8 Martyrdom of St Florian

Albrecht Altdorfer created this painting as part of a multipanel altar featuring scenes from the legend of St Florian. Other pieces from the series are in Florence.

4 Works of Master Theodoricus

Parts of an altar set on loan from Karlštejn Castle, are *St Luke, St Charlemagne, St Catherine, St Matthew, St Ambrose* and *St Gregory.*

5 Třeboň Altarpiece

Only three of the five double-sided panels of the 14th-century Třebon Altarpiece *(right)*have survived to the present day.

St Agnes

St Agnes of Bohemia was a powerful figure in medieval politics. Pope Gregory IX granted special privileges to her convent and his successor Innocent IV sent priceless relics to be housed there. Agnes died in 1282, but her influence on Czech statehood was felt centuries later when, in 1989, Pope John Paul II canonized her; five days later, the Velvet Revolution began (see p35).

Wenceslas Square

This former medieval horse market began to be redeveloped in the 19th century, fast becoming the commercial hub of Prague – in 1848 it was renamed Wenceslas Square, in honour of Bohemia's patron saint. The majority of the buildings seen today date from the early 20th century, and their beautiful Art Nouveau façades illustrate the embracing of this style by Czech architects of the time. Often the scene of historic events, the most recent was in 1989, when crowds gathered to celebrate the end of Communism (see p35).

St Wenceslas Statue and the National Museum

🄴 Enjoy the faded glory of the Hotel Evropa over a coffee in its charming café.

🄲 Owing to the high volume of tourists, Wenceslas Square is home to many pick-pockets. Be especially wary at the square's north end.

• Map N5

Top 10 Sights

1. National Museum
2. St Wenceslas Statue
3. Communist Memorial
4. Palác Lucerna
5. Palác Koruna
6. Hotel Evropa
7. Svobodné slovo Balcony
8. Franciscan Garden
9. Church of Our Lady of the Snows
10. St Wenceslas

OBĚTĚN

1 National Museum

Invading Warsaw Pact troops shelled the Neo-Renaissance building in 1968, assuming it was the Czechoslovak Parliament. The small entry fee is worth it, if only to see the museum's marble stairway *(above)* and pantheon of Czech cultural figures *(see p110)*.

2 St Wenceslas Statue

The Přemyslid prince sits astride a horse flanked by other Czech patrons *(below)* in Josef Myslbek's 1912 sculpture. The area "under the tail" is a traditional meeting place.

3 Communist Memorial

In front of St Wenceslas is a memorial to the victims of Communism *(below)*, such as the two men who died protesting against the Warsaw Pact invasion in 1968.

6 Hotel Evropa

It's gone to seed over the years, but the Art Nouveau building at No. 25 *(below)* preserves its original façade and some original decor *(see p78)*.

7 Svobodné slovo Balcony

During the Velvet Revolution *(see p35)*, Václav Havel addressed pro-democracy demonstrators from the balcony of the *Svobodné slovo* newspaper building. When the deposed Alexander Dubček joined him, the crowds knew that Communism was over.

8 Franciscan Garden

A stone's throw from the busy Wenceslas Square, this former monastery garden provides much-needed peace from the downtown bustle.

9 Church of Our Lady of the Snows

Founded by Charles IV on his coronation in 1347, this lovely church *(below)* was to have been more than 100 m (330 ft) long, but it was never completed.

10 St Wenceslas

Hanging in the central passage of the Palác Lucerna is David Černý's take on the Czech patron saint. Vandals repeatedly remove the horse's tongue.

Historic Demonstrations

Wenceslas Square saw its first demonstration in 1419 when Catholic reformer Jan Želivský led a procession to St Stephen's Church. On 28 October 1918 the area witnessed Czechoslovak independence. In 1969, Jan Palach set himself on fire here to protest against the Soviet occupation. It is still the scene of protests and victories today.

4 Palác Lucerna

President Václav Havel's grandfather designed and built this immense building on the square's western flank. It is now home to an art gallery, cinema, cafés, shops and a ballroom.

5 Palác Koruna

Built in "Geometric Modernist" style in 1912, this "palace" *(right)* became home to Turkish-style baths. It is now home to Koruna Palace Shopping Centre, which has many luxury stores.

⑩ Petřín Hill

Covered with forests, orchards and strolling lovers, Petřín Hill creates a soft counterpoint to the spires of Hradčany on the Vltava's left bank. Rising more than 300 m (1,000 ft) above sea level, the area began life as a vineyard in the 15th century, but has been a public park since 1825. Early chronicles say it was the site of pagan rituals to the god Perun, and believers still practise ancient rites here on 1 May each year. Above all, however, it is the perfect escape when the city crowds become too much to bear.

Strahov Stadium
2 It may be ugly, but Strahov Stadium *(above)* is the largest arena of its kind in the world. It was built for Sokol, a physical culture organization, and used for gymnastic rallies. Today it is a rock concert venue *(see p48)*.

Strahov Monastery façade

⊖ **Nebozízek restaurant (Petřínské sady 411) offers spectacular views of Prague.**

• Map C4
• *Observation Tower: Open Apr–Sep: 10am–10pm; Mar & Oct: 10am–8pm; Nov–Feb: 10am–6pm, Adm, Dis. access*
• *Strahov Monastery; www.strahovsky klaster.cz; Open 9am–noon, 1–5pm daily, Adm*
• *Mirror Maze: Open Apr–Sep: 10am–10pm; Mar & Oct: 10am–8pm; Nov–Feb: 10am–6pm, Adm, Dis. access*
• *Church of St Michael, Church of St Lawrence: Closed to the public (except during masses Sun, Mon or Fri)*
• *Štefánik's Observatory: Opening timings vary throughout the year, Adm, Dis. access*
• *Funicular; www.dpp. cz; Open 9am–11:30pm daily, Adm Kč24*

Top 10 Features

1 Observation Tower
2 Strahov Stadium
3 Strahov Monastery
4 Mirror Maze
5 Hunger Wall
6 Karel Hynek Mácha Statue
7 Church of St Michael
8 Štefánik's Observatory
9 Church of St Lawrence
10 Funicular

Observation Tower
1 Modelled after the Eiffel Tower in Paris, Petřín Hill's *Eiffelovka* stands only one-quarter as high as its inspiration, at 63.5 m (210 ft). It was created for the Jubilee Exposition of 1891. A climb of 299 stairs leads to the viewing platform.

Strahov Monastery
3 Founded in 1140, Strahov houses the nation's oldest books in the Strahov Library while still functioning as a monastery. The Theological Hall, with its frescoes and statue of St John *(above)*, is a must-see.

For more parks and gardens in Prague See pp40–41

Mirror Maze
After laughing at the distorting mirrors in the labyrinth, take in a bit of history with a diorama depicting the final battle of the Thirty Years' War on Charles Bridge *(below)*.

Karel Hynek Mácha Statue
Mácha is a national poet, best loved for his Romantic poem "May". On 1 May, young lovers lay flowers at his statue's feet *(above)*.

Štefánik's Observatory
Operating since 1928, the observatory was named after M.R. Štefánik, who was a Slovak diplomat and co-founder of the Czechoslovakian state, as well as a scientist and astronomer.

Church of St Lawrence
Facing the labyrinth is the onion-domed Church of St Lawrence, built on a pagan shrine in the 10th century. It was rebuilt in Baroque style in the 18th century.

Funicular
If you want to save your breath, do as visitors have done since 1890 and take the funicular railway to the top of the hill and walk down. The cable car offers outstanding views of the castle to the north.

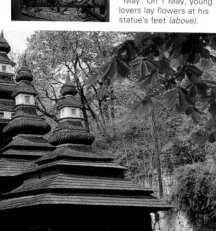

Hunger Wall
The 14th-century wall *(below)* was originally part of the city's southern fortifications. Charles IV is said to have ordered its construction as a public works project to feed the poor during a famine.

Church of St Michael
Still used for services, this lovely wooden church *(above)* was moved to Prague when the Ukraine valley it stood in was flooded by a dammed river.

Strahov Monastery Exhibits

Since its founding in the 12th century, Strahov Monastery has suffered fires, pillaging armies and totalitarian regimes. Josef II dissolved most local monasteries in 1783, but spared Strahov on the condition that the monks conduct research at their library. The majority of the research at the Strahov Library today involves preserving the paper and preventing it from being devoured by acidity. On display in the Theological and Philosophical Halls are old books, ornate gospels, miniature Bibles and a picture gallery.

Left **Charles IV** Right *Encampment of Matthias*, Rudolph II's brother, 1608

🔟 Moments in History

1 Wenceslas Assassinated

The "Good King" (actually a prince) was the second Christian ruler of Czech lands, succeeding his grandfather Bořivoj. Wenceslas solidified ties with Rome and with German merchants. Murdered by his brother in 935, he was later canonized.

2 Charles IV Becomes Holy Roman Emperor

Grandson of an emperor and son of a Přemyslid princess, Charles could hardly help rising to both the Roman and Bohemian thrones in 1333. Prague became the seat of imperial power under his reign, as well as an archbishopric and the home of central Europe's first university.

3 Hussite Wars

After the Church Council at Constance burned Catholic reformer Jan Hus at the stake in 1415 *(see p15)*, his followers literally beat their ploughshares into swords and rebelled against both church and crown. The resulting animosity between Protestant Czechs and German Catholics would rage for centuries.

4 Reign of Rudolph II

The melancholy emperor (1576–1611) was not much good as a statesman and was under threat from his ambitious brother, Matthias, but he was a liberal benefactor of the arts and sciences. Among his achievements were the support of Johannes Kepler's studies of planetary motion. He also promoted religious freedom.

5 Battle of White Mountain

The Protestant nobility and the emperor continued to provoke each other until hostilities broke into open war. Imperial forces devastated the Czechs in the first battle of the Thirty Years' War in 1620. Czech lands were re-Catholicized, but resentment against Vienna and Rome continued to smoulder.

6 Independence

While World War I raged, National Revival leaders such as Tomáš Masaryk turned to the United States for support for an independent Czechoslovakia. As the war drew to a close in 1918, the republic of Czechoslovakia was born.

Battle of White Mountain

7 World War II
The First Republic had barely stretched its legs when the Munich Agreement of 1938 gave Czech lands to Nazi Germany. Nearly 80,000 Czechs died in the Holocaust *(see p25)*. After the war, the nation exacted revenge by expelling its German citizens.

Nazi parade, Wenceslas Square, 1939

8 Rise of Communism
Grateful to the Red Army for liberating Prague in 1945, Czechoslovakia gave Soviet Communism the benefit of the doubt in the February 1948 elections.

9 Prague Spring
In 1968 First Secretary Alexandr Dubček introduced economic and social reforms that did not sit well with Moscow. Warsaw-Pact tanks rolled through Prague streets killing more than 100 protestors.

10 Velvet Revolution
After 10 days of mass protests in 1989, the Communist government bowed to the population's indignation. Czechs proudly recall that not a window was broken during the revolt.

Velvet Revolution celebrations

Top 10 Historical Figures

1 St Agnes
St Agnes (1211–82), devout sister of Wenceslas I, built a convent for the order of the Poor Clares (the female counterpart of the Franciscans).

2 St John of Nepomuk
Wenceslas IV arrested Nepomuk (1340–93) over the election of an abbot and threw his body from Charles Bridge.

3 Jan Hus
Hus (1370–1415) preached against Church corruption and was burned as a heretic.

4 Mordecai Maisel
The Jewish mayor (1528–1601) was one of the richest men in Europe *(see p22)*.

5 Tycho de Brahe
Astronomer at Rudolph's court, Brahe (1546–1601) suffered a burst bladder when he refused to leave the emperor's side at a banquet.

6 Edward Kelley and John Dee
The English charlatans gained Rudolph II's trust by converting lead into gold, but were more interested in necromancy.

7 Johannes Kepler
The German astronomer (1571–1630) pioneered studies of planetary motion.

8 Albrecht von Wallenstein
Leader of the Catholics during the Thirty Years' War, Wallenstein (1583–1634) built a vast palace in Prague *(see p86)*.

9 Franz Kafka
Prague's best-known author (1883–1924) was largely unpublished in his lifetime *(see p44)*.

10 Emil Zátopek
"The Locomotive" (1922–2000) won three long-distance gold medals at the 1952 Olympic Games.

 Flooding in August 2002 caused a great deal of damage to many historic landmarks in Prague.

Left **National Gallery** Right **Prague Municipal Gallery**

🔟 Museums and Galleries

National Gallery

The National Gallery's extensive art collection is spread throughout the city in six separate locations. Kinský Palace holds the prints and drawings collection; St Agnes's Convent *(see pp28–9)*, medieval art; Sternberg Palace, the Old Masters; the Trade Fair Palace, the modern and contemporary collections *(see pp26–7)*; Schwarzenberg Palace, Baroque art and Salmovský Palace holds temporary exhibitions. ◈ *Kinský Palace: Staroměstské náměstí 12, Map M3 • Sternberg Palace, Salmovský Palace: Hradčanské náměstí 15, Map B2 • Schwarzenberg Palace: Hradčanské náměstí 2, Map B2 • Trade Fair Palace: Dukelských hrdinů 47, Map M3 • Open 10am–6pm Tue–Sun • Adm*

National Museum

The National Museum's collections are spread throughout the country, but the flagship site is

Statue of Music, Galerie Rudolfinum

the historical and natural history collections housed in the Neo-Renaissance building at the top of Wenceslas Square *(see p110)*.

Galerie Rudolfinum

The "House of Artists" hosts a wide range of temporary exhibitions, each running for several months. If you're at all a fan of contemporary art, it's always worth a visit, whatever aspect they are covering at the time. ◈ *Alšovo nábřeží 12 • Map K2 • 227 059205 for tours • Dis. access • Adm*

Smetana Museum

The grand Renaissance style building, formerly owned by a water company, houses the museum dedicated to the father of Czech music, Bedřich Smetana. Documents, letters, scores and instruments detailing the composer's life and work are exhibited here. ◈ *Novotného lávka 1 • Map J5 • 222 220082 • Open 10am–5pm Wed–Mon • Adm*

National Museum

Prague Municipal Gallery

The House of the Golden Ring, the House at the Stone Bell and the Old Town Hall *(see pp16–17)* are used for temporary exhibitions of 19th- and 20th-century Czech art. Permanent exhibitions can be found in the Troja Château *(see p120)*.

◈ House at the Golden Ring: Týnská 6, Map M3, Open 10am–6pm Tue–Sun, Adm • House at the Stone Bell: Staroměstské náměstí 13, Map M3, Open 10am–8pm Tue–Sun, Adm • www.ghmp.cz

Montanelli Museum

This contemporary art gallery holds the collection of the DrAK Foundation, as well as a variety of imaginative modern works created by local and foreign artists. There are also educational programmes for children and regular guided tours in English. ◈ Nerudova 13 • Map C2 • 257 531220 • Open noon–6pm daily • Adm • Dis. access • www. muzeummontanelli.com

The Smetana Museum

Carved chest, Museum of Decorative Arts

Jewish Museum

The museum's collection of Judaic art is perhaps the world's largest, while other exhibits present the lives and history of Jews in Bohemia and Moravia. The collection is spread out around the synagogues of Josefov *(see pp98–101)*.

Museum of Decorative Arts

The museum has spiced up its collection of crystal, porcelain and woodcarving with exhibitions of Czech fashion and other shows. ◈ 17. listopadu 2 • Map L2 • 251 093111 • Open 10am–6pm Wed–Sun, until 7pm Tue • Adm

National Technical Museum

The ultimate how-things-work museum, with exhibitions on mining, telecommunications and transport. Get a guide to show you the coal mine in the basement. ◈ Kostelní 42 • Map M3 • Open 9am–5:30pm Tue–Fri, 10am–6pm Sat–Sun • Adm • Dis. access

Public Transport Museum

A celebration of more than 100 years of Prague's transport systems, from horse-drawn carriages to the metro.
◈ Patočkova 4 • Map A1 • Open Apr–Nov: 9am–5pm Sat–Sun • Adm

CHARD13.XII1890 MALVINA &VII.900.16.XII...DOLF...
11942 SAMUEL14.XI1896.2ZII1942 SAMSON...VII1872 RNOS
VII1904.18XII1943 VLADIMÍR9.VII1908-26...941 ...ENĚ....V19
5.VI1875.19X1942 ARNOŠTKA21.V1901...1944 BEDŘIŠKA21
ILIE2.III1913.12.X1944 EVA5.XI1919 ANA29.I.V1959.JIŘÍ TOMÁŠ16.
XI1921.1C.V11942 HERMINA10.IV1877.10.VII1942 IDA29.V1864.27...
2.11859.19X1942 KATEŘINA4.VIII1864.19.X1942...LÁRA13.IX1E

Left **Holocaust wall, Pinkas Synagogue** Right **Monument, Cathedral of Sts Cyril and Methodius**

🔟 Places of Worship

1 St Vitus's Cathedral

The current building, looming majestically over the castle complex, is a combination of architectural styles and took more than 600 years to complete. In days of old, the cathedral was the setting of spectacular Bohemian coronations by Prague's archbishops. It's also the final resting place of the saints Wenceslas, John of Nepomuk and scores of other Czech worthies (see pp12–13).

2 Old-New Synagogue

Prague's Orthodox Jewish community still holds services in this 13th-century synagogue – the oldest in Central Europe. The building's curious name may come from the Hebrew *Al-Tenai*, meaning "with reservation". Legend has it that its stones will eventually have to be returned to Jerusalem, from whence they came (see pp24–5).

Virgin Mary statue, Loreto

Madonna, Church of Our Lady Before Týn

3 Loreto

At the heart of this elaborate shrine to the Virgin Mary is the Santa Casa – a reproduction of the house where Mary received the Angel Gabriel. The Loreto treasury holds scores of priceless monstrances as well as other religious artifacts (see pp20–21).

4 Church of Our Lady Before Týn

The Gothic towers of Týn loom over Old Town Square's houses. During the Counter-Reformation, the Jesuits melted down the gold Hussite chalice that stood between the towers and recast it as the Madonna seen today (see p14). Ⓢ Staroměstské náměstí 14 • Map M3 • Open 10am–1pm & 3–5pm Tue–Sat, 10:30am–noon Sun • Dis. access

5 Church of our Lady Victorious

This Baroque church contains the famed statue of the Infant Jesus of Prague. The wax baby doll is credited with miraculous powers. The resident Order of English Virgins look after the little man and change his clothes (see p83).

Moorish decoration, Spanish Synagogue

St Nicholas Church
The Malá Strana church's cartoon-like clock tower and dome upstage its namesake across the river. The splendid Baroque sanctuary was meant to impress Catholic sceptics of the might of Rome (see p82).

Spanish Synagogue
The present Moorish building with its opulent interior replaced Prague's oldest synagogue after the latter was razed in 1867. The Conservative Jewish community holds services here. It also houses Jewish Museum exhibits, offices and a reference centre (see p101).

Pinkas Synagogue
The names of approximately 80,000 Czech victims of the Holocaust cover the walls of this house adjacent to the Old Jewish Cemetery, as an emotive memorial (see p25). The women's gallery was added in the 18th century (see p101).

Church of St James
The Baroque façade is awash with cherubim and scenes from the lives of saints Francis of Assisi, James and Antony of Padua. It's an active house of worship, so gaze respectfully at the mummified arm hanging above the door inside (see p74).

Cathedral of Sts Cyril and Methodius
Nazi *Reichsprotektor* Reinhard "The Hangman" Heydrich's assassins (see p106) took refuge in this Eastern Orthodox Cathedral's crypt. The Gestapo executed the bishop who sheltered them. ◐
Resslova 9 • Map E5 • Open Mar–Oct: 9am–5pm Tue–Sun; Nov–Feb: 9am–5pm Tue–Sat • Dis. access • Adm

Cathedral of Sts Cyril and Methodius

Left **Funicular, Petřín Hill** Right **Kampa Island**

🔟 Parks and Gardens

1 Petřín Hill
The views from here are so beautiful that susceptible romantics have been known to spontaneously kiss passers-by, including the monks from Strahov monastery. They are best in spring when the orchards are in bloom *(see pp32–3)*.

2 Vyšehrad
Far enough from the centre to be largely tourist-free, Vyšehrad is the perfect place to be alone with your thoughts. Sights include the Neo-Gothic Church of Sts Peter and Paul, the graves of Dvořák and Smetana and reconstructed fortifications. There's very little shelter from inclement weather *(see p121)*.

3 Wallenstein Garden
General Albrecht von Wallenstein razed two dozen houses to make way for his expansive "backyard". Among

Stromovka

the garden's stranger elements is the grotesquery on the southern wall, with stalactites imitating a limestone cave. The cries you hear all around you are the resident peacocks *(see p83)*.

4 Kampa Island
Malá Strana residents love to sunbathe, sip wine and play frisbee on the island green of the Little Quarter in summer. However, they also like to smoke marijuana, beat drums well into the night and use the grass for a public dog toilet, so watch your step *(see p82)*.

Wallenstein Garden

5 Vojanovy sady
Prague's oldest garden was founded in the 13th century. It is home to peacocks, fruit trees and a heart-melting array of flowers *(see p83).*

6 Stromovka
Otakar II established the royal hunting park here in 1266. A public garden since 1804, its ponds are ideal for ice-skating in winter and duck-feeding in summer. Its meandering paths offer easy strolling *(see p116).*

7 Franciscan Garden
Stop here after pounding the Wenceslas Square pavement and join the pensioners and office workers at lunch, quietly filling the benches behind the Church of Our Lady of the Snows *(see p105).*

8 Prague Castle Royal Garden
These formal gardens were laid out by Ferdinand I in the 16th century. After mulling over the Belvedere summer palace and the Communist-revised frescoes on the Ball-Game Hall, slip down to the Stag Moat *(see pp8–11).*

9 Střelecký Island
Lose yourself watching the Vltava rush past. Early risers can watch the sunrise strike the castle. In summer there's a popular outdoor cinema and live-music stage here. ◉ *Map D4*

10 South Gardens of Prague Castle
The spectacular views of Malá Strana from this series of gardens descending from Prague Castle can't fail to inspire. This really is the best way to conclude a day of sightseeing at Hradčany *(see pp8–11).*

South Gardens of Prague Castle

41

Left **The Golden Key** Right **The Red Lamb**

🔟 House Signs

1 The White Swan
Prague houses weren't given identifying numbers until 1770. Empress Maria Theresa was a great one for bringing the famed Habsburg trait of orderliness from Vienna to the banks of the Vltava. Before that, homes were known and located by a charming but confusing system of allegorical symbols. Although you can still find such emblematic addresses throughout the older parts of the city, Nerudova street in Malá Strana *(see p81)* has the highest concentration of house signs in the city. Originally many of them had alchemical significance, although today much of their meaning has been lost. The White Swan is one of these, and probably originated as a golden goose (not to be confused with the downtown department store of the same name, Bílá Labut'). ◈ *Nerudova 49*

2 The Two Suns
This house was the birthplace of the much-loved Czech poet and author Jan Neruda (1834–91), after whom the street is named. Traditionally this was the writers' and artists' area of Prague, and Neruda conveyed the Bohemian atmosphere of Malá Strana in his work. The connection continues today with the quarter's many small art galleries and craft shops. ◈ *Nerudova 47*

3 The Golden Key
Castle goldsmiths, such as the ones who worked at this house in the 17th century, paid fees to the city, unlike their colleagues who lived in the castle's Golden Lane *(see p9)*. As such, they were entitled to advertise their wares, as preserved today in this building's façade. ◈ *Nerudova 27*

The Two Suns

4 The Red Lamb
One of the street's more unlikely symbols, the scarlet sheep adorning this façade has an alchemical significance so arcane, not even the current house owner can explain it. Not that it matters – it remains in place as one of the city's many charming idiosyncrasies. ◈ *Nerudova 11*

Apart from studying its beautiful house signs, Nerudova is a convenient route from the Old Town to Prague Castle.

St Wenceslas's Horse

in some quarters – are more interested in the meditative aspects of the art, however. ◈ *Nerudova 28*

The Three Fiddles
They say a demonic trio screeches on their instruments here on moonlit nights. The house was home to a family of violin-makers in the early 18th century, and the sign advertised their trade. Like many of the other buildings on this street, it is now home to a restaurant. ◈ *Nerudova 12*

The Devil
Lucifer pops up as a cuddly character on houses all over town and in local legend, more a folksy trickster than a sinister prince of darkness. Here, he'll tempt you to dine at a not completely infernal restaurant. ◈ *Nerudova 4*

The Green Lobster
Who knows what they were thinking when they hung the crustacean above their door. Probably trying to keep up with the neighbours at the Pendant Parsnip at No. 39. ◈ *Nerudova 43*

St Wenceslas's Horse
Clearly seen on the Old Town Square on the façade of Štorch House, this is a tribute both to the patron saint of Bohemia and the blacksmiths who shod horses bound for the castle. ◈ *Staroměstské náměstí*

The Three Lillies
Although their image no longer adorns the façade, the three flowers remain atop the house. The house also lends its name to a feverish tale of passion and thunderstorms by Jan Neruda. Many of the author's tales were set in houses such as this one. ◈ *Nerudova 15*

The Golden Wheel
Another alchemical symbol, the wheel represents a stage in the *magnum opus*, the process by which lead was purportedly turned into gold. Modern day alchemists – yes, they still exist

The Three Fiddles

Left **Karel Čapek** Centre **Franz Kafka and his fiancé** Right **Václav Havel**

TOP 10 Writers and Composers

1 Franz Kafka
Although he wrote in German and almost none of his work was published in his lifetime, Franz Kafka *is* Prague. Many of his disturbing novels seem to foresee the Communist years. His peripatetic wanderings across this city, brooding features and death by tuberculosis all add to the mystique.

2 Gustav Meyrink
Almost completely unknown outside Austria, Meyrink is nevertheless responsible for one of the city's most marketable notions: the Golem. He penned the story of the clay monster, that was supposedly locked up in the Old-New Synagogue, in 1915 and attributed its creation to the real Rabbi Loew *(see p52)*.

3 Karel Čapek
This Czech writer is best known for his science fiction and psychologically penetrating novels. With his 1920 play *R.U.R. (Rossum's Universal Robots)* he gave the world a word for an automaton, based on a Czech word for "forced labour".

4 Jaroslav Hašek
A notorious joker and the author of the celebrated dig at the Austrian army, *The Adventures of the Good Soldier Švejk)*, Hašek was also the creator of the satirical Party for Moderate Progress Within the Bounds of the Law.

5 Wolfgang Amadeus Mozart
Prague and Vienna continue to duel over the musical genius's legacy, with the Czechs always claiming that Mozart loved them better. The composer premiered his opera *Don Giovanni* in Prague's Estates Theatre *(see p65)* and Prague residents mourned spectacularly upon his death in 1791. Regular Mozart concerts are held in the city.

6 Bedřich Smetana
The composer wrote his opera *Libuše*, based on the legendary princess, for the reopening of Prague's National Theatre in 1883. Smetana vies with Antonín Dvořák for the title of best-loved Czech composer; the former's ode to beer in *The Bartered Bride* gives him a certain advantage.

Wolfgang Amadeus Mozart

Antonín Dvořák

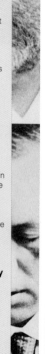

Top 10 Works of Art, Music and Literature

1 The Trial
The protagonist Joseph K. of Kafka's 1925 novel finds himself accused of a crime he did not commit.

2 The Castle
Kafka worked on this novel of social alienation while living in Prague Castle's Golden Lane (see p9).

3 Adventures of the Good Soldier Švejk
Hašek was so effective in sending up the army and the Austro-Hungarian empire that Czechs still have a hard time taking authority seriously.

4 Slavonic Epic
Art Nouveau master Alfons Mucha celebrates the Czech mythic past in this artwork.

5 R.U.R.
Čapek's science-fiction play is a study of labour relations and social structures.

6 Grandmother
Author Božena Němcová based the narrator on her own grandmother, from whom she heard many of these stories.

7 Vltava
Smetana's *My Country* are six tone poems celebrating Bohemia. The second follows the river's course.

8 New World Symphony
With his 1893 ninth symphony, Dvořák incorporated the style of black folk songs.

9 Disturbing the Peace
Havel meditates on Communism and the values underlying Central Europe's pursuit of democracy.

10 The Unbearable Lightness of Being
Kundera's non-linear tale of love, politics and the betrayals inherent in both.

7 Antonín Dvořák
Dvořák's works, such as his *Slavonic Dances*, regularly incorporate folk music. He composed his final *New World Symphony* while he was director of the National Conservatory in New York City.

8 Bohumil Hrabal
The poetic author used to sit in the Old Town pub U Zlatého tygra (see p60), taking down the stories he heard there. He died falling from his hospital-room window in 1997.

9 Václav Havel
The Czech president was known as a playwright before he became a civil rights activist protesting the Warsaw Pact invasion in 1968 (see p35). His absurdist works and his fame helped draw international attention to his country's struggles.

10 Milan Kundera
Czechs have a love-hate relationship with their best-known contemporary author. Since his emigration to France, Kundera has had little to do with his native country, even writing his novels in French. His works convey a comic skepticism.

Left **Mission: Impossible** Right **Kolya**

TOP 10 Film Locations

Amadeus

1 Amadeus

As a drunken Wolfgang Amadeus Mozart, Tom Hulce staggered through Malá Strana's narrow Thunovská alley in Miloš Forman's Academy Award-winning 1984 interpretation of Peter Shaffer's successful play. Prague was a well chosen location for the film, since Mozart's *Don Giovanni* debuted at the Estates Theatre *(see p65)*, and Praguers are intensely proud of the association.

2 The Unbearable Lightness of Being

Daniel Day Lewis and Juliette Binoche played an unhappily married couple living on Radnické schody during the 1968 Warsaw Pact invasion, in the 1988 film adaptation of Milan Kundera's dark novel about love, relationships and betrayal *(see p45)*.

3 Mission: Impossible

Cars explode on Kampa Island, restaurants explode on the Old Town Square. The opulent party in the thriller's opening scene takes place in the National Museum, in this 1996 sci-fi fantasy starring Tom Cruise.

4 Les Misérables

Jean Valjean, played by Liam Neeson, fled from the *gendarme* on Hradčanské náměstí through Prague sewers in the 1998 remake of this classic tale. Neeson also fled from fans at Molly Malone's Irish pub.

5 The Shooter

In a chase scene, Dolph Lundgren leaps from a rooftop at Prague Castle and lands, miraculously, on the National Theatre; Prague audiences were unimpressed by this lack of authenticity in 1995.

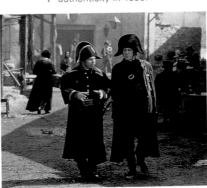

Les Misérables

Discover more at **www.traveldk.com**

The Unbearable Lightness of Being

6 From Hell
The Hughes brothers turned Saská Alley near Charles Bridge and other Malá Strana locations into Jack the Ripper's foggy London in 2001. Off-screen, Johnny Depp retreated to the smoky depths of the Blue Light bar on Josefská.

7 Plunkett and Macleane
Jonny Lee Miller and Robert Carlyle blunderbuss their way up and down Thunovská. Locals were used as 18th-century extras for the 1999 production.

8 Kolya
In 1996 Jan Svěrák cast his father Zdeněk as the grumpy, philandering cellist who restores Olšanská cemetery tombstones in his free time. The five-year-old title character gets lost in Anděl metro station *(see p49)*.

9 The Bourne Identity
Jindřišská and Panská near Wenceslas Square serve as Zurich in this 2002 film adaptation of Robert Ludlum's novel.

10 The Chronicles of Narnia: Prince Caspian
In 2007 sets for Miraz's Castle and the underground hiding places of the Narnians were created at Barrandov Studios.

Top 10 Czech Filmmakers

1 Miloš Forman
The Academy Award-winning director of *One Flew Over the Cuckoo's Nest* (1975) returned to his homeland to film *Amadeus*.

2 Jan Svěrák
This young director is carrying Czech filmmaking into the 21st century with films such as *Kolya* (1996).

3 Jan and Eva Švankmajer
Director Jan creates films in which his wife Eva's Surrealist animated objects come to life.

4 Gene Deitch
Deitch was a little-known animator before he took a job producing films in Communist Czechoslovakia. He fell in love with the city and stayed.

5 Gustav Machatý
When a young Slovak actress took off her clothes in Machatý's *Ecstasy* (1932) it became the first film to feature nudity; the actress became Hedy Lamarr.

6 Petr Zelenka
This young turk focuses on oddballs in films such as *Loners* (2000).

7 Jiří Menzel
Menzel won the country's first Academy Award with *Closely Watched Trains*.

8 Věra Chytilová
The *grande dame* of Czech cinematography – her best film is *Daisies* (1966).

9 Karel Vachek
Vachek creates rambling documentaries which capture the absurdity of Czech politics.

10 Ivan Reitman
Reitman, now US-based, is best known for directing the hit *Ghostbusters*.

Prague's Top 10

47

Left **Strahov Stadium** Right **Anděl Metro Station**

TOP 10 Communist Monuments

1 Žižkov TV Tower

The city's most hated building among Praguers was built in 1985–92, and was intended, according to rumour, to jam foreign radio signals or emit nefarious radiation. Despite its utilitarian design, however, the view of Prague's skyline from the top of the 216-m (709-ft) tower is spectacular on a clear day *(see p117)*.

2 National Memorial on the Vítkov Hill

After a failed attempt to embalm President Klement Gottwald after his death in 1953, the Communist government was forced to cremate their favoured leader. His ashes, as well as those of various other *apparatchiks*, were buried here atop Vítkov Hill, behind the giant statue of Jan Žižka. They were removed after the Velvet Revolution *(see p35)*. Today the monument serves as a museum of Czech and Czechoslovak history. ◈ *Vítkov Hill, Žižkov • Map B6 • Open 10am–6pm Wed–Sun*

3 Strahov Stadium

Prague Castle would fit inside this massive arena situated on Petřín Hill. Built in 1955 for the purposes of *spartakiáda* physical culture performances, the structure was the first concrete panel building in Czechoslovakia. Today, the stadium serves as a training centre for the AC Sparta football team. Some popular bands have also held performances here, much to the delight of local kids *(see p32)*.

4 Letná Plinth

Where sculptor V. Karel Novák's giant metronome now swings once stood a massive, 14,000-ton statue of Joseph Stalin – the largest in the world – backed by a queue of admiring citizens. The statue was visible from all over the city. Stalin's successor Nikita Khrushchev had the statue destroyed by a series of dramatic dynamite explosions in 1962. Pop star Michael Jackson launched his 1996 World Tour in Prague, unwisely erecting a statue of himself on the very same spot. ◈ *Letenské sady, Letná • Map E1*

Sbratření

Czech Radio Building

Congress Centre

5 Since its partial reconstruction in 2000, this is one of the most modern congress centres in Europe. The excellent acoustics in the Congress Hall make this one of the best concert venues in the world, comparable to the famous halls of London, Montreal and Boston. The centre has capacity for close to 10,000 visitors *(see p121)*.

Anděl Metro Station

6 In the reconstruction of the Anděl Centre, developers removed an epic mosaic tribute to the friendship between Moscow and Prague, but from the metro platforms below, you can still see frieze tributes to Soviet cosmonauts. Even if you're not riding the metro, you need a standard ticket to access the platform. ◈ *Map A6*

Sbratření

7 This bronze statue recalls the Red Army's liberation of Prague in 1945: a grateful resistance fighter greets a Soviet footsoldier with a bunch of lilac and a, presumably brotherly, kiss. It's one of the few pro-Soviet monuments still standing in Prague. ◈ *Vrchlického sady • Map G4*

Czech Radio Building

8 Warsaw-Pact tanks invaded the Czech capital in 1968 to put an end to Alexander Dubček's Prague Spring liberalization. Among those who paid for their resistance with their lives were Czech Radio journalists, who first broadcast the news that the nation was under attack. A plaque in front of the building honours their bravery. ◈ *Vinohradská 12, Vinohrady • Map B6 • Closed to the public*

New Building of the National Museum

9 From its construction in the 1970s until Czechoslovakia split into Czech and Slovak republics in 1993, this was the Federal Assembly building, and later Radio Free Europe (1994–2009). Today, the building houses several temporary exhibitions but is still in the process of being named. ◈ *Vinohradská 1, New Town • Map H5 • Open 10am–6pm daily • Adm*

Museum of Communism

10 This museum seeks to help visitors experience totalitarianism first-hand through reproductions and genuine objects from the Communist era. The most chilling area is the reconstructed interrogation room. Although locals might not agree, the tour is more fun than it sounds *(see p110)*.

Museum of Communism

Left **Poster, Wax Museum Praha** Right **The Magic Flute**

🔟 Eccentric Prague

1 Museum of Torture Instruments

If you can't quite grasp how these grisly instruments work, the helpful illustrations should make their operation painfully clear. More than 60 implements of pain from all over Europe are on display, accompanied by explanations in four languages. ⊗ *Křižovnické náměstí 1 • Map J4 • Open 10am–10pm daily (to 8pm in winter) • Adm*

2 Rock Therapy

Subtitled "a Small Story From the Great Time of the Beatles", this non-verbal show uses film projection, music, dance and puppetry to present "a loosely poetical black-theatrical production of the animated film *Yellow Submarine*". It is, if nothing else, a unique synthesis of various Czech theatre genres. Must be seen to be believed, whether you're a Beatles fan or not. ⊗ *Animato Theater, Na Příkopě 10 • Map N5 • Adm*

3 Wax Museum Praha

Bohemia's great figures all come together in one happy community here, with lifelike waxwork representations of Franz Kafka, Rudolf II and The Good Soldier Švejk, making for a wonderful stroll through Czech history. The presence of Bill Clinton, Elton John, Tina Turner and other modern icons is a little more difficult to fathom. ⊗ *Celetná 6 • Map M4 • Open 10am–9pm daily • Adm*

4 Marionette Don Giovanni

Mozart premiered his opera *Don Giovanni* at Prague's Estates Theatre in 1787. Of the two marionette homages to the city's favourite opera, the better production takes place at the National Marionette Theatre. The technique of the puppeteers is so masterful, you'll leave looking for strings attached to passers-by. A true Prague experience *(see p65).*

Museum of Torture Instruments

5 Choco-Story Museum

This chocoholic's delight is based on the well-known Chocolate Museum in Bruges, Belgium, and showcases the 2,600-year history of this delicacy, from the discovery of cocoa to modern production methods. Visitors will also get the chance

Choco-Story Museum

to learn the secret of producing silky chocolate and to sample products made on the spot.
⑨ *Celetná 10 • Map M4 • Open 10am–7pm daily • Adm*

Sex Machine Museum

An exhibition in a slightly different sense, this is one show definitely not for the kids. The museum traces the history of gratifying instruments from their origins to the modern day. While not entirely without cultural merit, the overall package is rather bizarre. There is, predictably, a gift shop. ⑨ *Melantrichova 18 • Map L4 • Open 10am–11pm daily • Adm*

Křižík Fountain

Each summer evening, the fountain's 50 pumps, 3,000 water jets and more than 1,200 lights put on a dizzying display of hydro-mechanic choreography. The musical accompaniment ranges from classical to heavy metal to Disney tunes. Productions have included live folk dance troupes and a melodrama based on James Bond plots *(see p116)*.
⑨ *Výstaviště, Holešovice • Map B5*

McGee's Ghost Tours

Whether you are a believer, a sceptic, interested in the unexplained or simply looking for an entertaining evening, guides will take you through narrow lanes and cobbled alleys, to the ancient churches and monuments, where you will hear about alchemists, murderers and unfortunate souls who lived there. ⑨ *Týnská 7 • Map M3*

The Magic Flute

W.A. Mozart's last opera, this magical fairytale *singspiel* is a classic in a new playful concept of figure and puppet theatre. The story of Prince Tamino and Princess Pamina is full of humour and fantasy and has been entertaining viewers for over 200 years. ⑨ *National Marionette Theatre: Žatecká 1 • Map L3*

Operetta

The Czech love of operetta knows no limits, except perhaps the number of performers willing to take part in the latest rock opera at locations around town.

It began with *Romany and Juliette*, proceeded to *Dracula* and is still going strong with a romping *Monte Cristo*. Check *The Prague Post* for performance times *(see p128)*. ⑨ *Divadlo Broadway: Na Příkopě 31; Map N5 • Divadlo Ta Fantastika: Karlova 8; Map L4• Hudební Divadlo Karlín Křižíkova 10; Map H2*

Křižík Fountain

Left **The Golem** Centre **One-Armed Thief** Right **Emaus Monastery**

🔟 Haunted Places

1 Mysteriae Pragensis
Uncover old Prague's most famous mysteries and legends in this museum exploring the city's ghosts and stories. Spread over two floors, the atmospheric cellar features a replica of some of old Prague's streets, while the ground floor offers more traditional exhibits explaining the background to the legends. All of the material on show is based on authentic records. ⓢ Mostecká 18 • Map C3

2 Turk in Ungelt
Among the merchants who lived in the Týn settlement behind the Church of Our Lady (see p14) was a Turkish immigrant. When his betrothed ran off and married another, he flew into a rage and chopped her head off. He is said to wander around the Ungelt court-yard carrying the decapitated head.

3 One-Armed Thief
Rumour has it that a thief sought to steal jewels from a statue of the Madonna in the Church of St James (see p74), but the stony Virgin seized him by the arm and local butchers had to cut him loose. According to some, he still haunts the church asking visitors to help him fetch his arm, which hangs from the wall inside.

4 The Golem
Legend has it that Rabbi Loew created a clay robot to help out around the house. When the creature raised a ruckus, Loew was forced to deactivate him and stashed him in the attic of the Old-New Synagogue (see p24).

5 The Iron Man
Believing his fiancée had been untrue, a knight called off his wedding. After she drowned herself in grief, he realized his mistake and hanged himself. Every 100 years he "appears" in Platnéřská Street, hoping to find a young virgin who will free him by talking to him for at least an hour.

6 The Drowned Man
When the bicycle was all the rage in the late 19th century, young Boběř Říma stole one and rode it into the river. If a soggy young fellow tries to sell you a bike near the Old Town end of Charles Bridge, just keep walking.

7 Emaus Devil
In an attempt to bedevil the monks at the Emaus Monastery, Satan took a job there as a cook and seasoned their food with pepper and other spices. To this day, Czech cuisine has few piquant flavours.

The Iron Man

Werewolf

8 Werewolf

Apparently, Rudolph II's gamekeeper became so enamoured with the wolves that roamed the castle's Stag Moat that he became one himself. Nowadays, he takes the form of a large dog and tends to chase cyclists, joggers and tourists when the whim takes him, so keep looking over your shoulder.

9 Drahomíra

St Wenceslas's mother was, by all accounts, an unpleasant woman. She killed her mother-in-law and might have done in her son, too, but the gates of hell swallowed her up before she could act. She sometimes wheels through Loretánská náměstí in a fiery carriage.

10 The Mad Barber

When a local barber foresook his home and family after he became caught up in alchemical pursuits, his daughters ended up in a brothel and his wife killed herself. He is said to haunt the vicinity of Karlova and Liliova streets, hoping to return to his honest profession and make amends.

Top 10 False Stories

1 Czechs are Christian
According to the last census, almost 59 per cent of Czechs proclaimed to be atheists.

2 Vyšehrad Castle
Vyšehrad was the first seat of power, but its importance has been inflated by legend.

3 Alchemists Lived in Golden Lane
Alchemists tended to live on credit in houses in town.

4 Jan Nepomuk Died on Charles Bridge
Nepomuk was already dead when he was thrown over the side *(see p19)*.

5 Jan Masaryk Committed Suicide
In 1948 the Foreign Minister was found dead in front of Černín Palace, having "fallen" from a window, according to the Communists.

6 There's Only One Bud
The town of České Budějovice (Budweis in German) was producing beer before the US brewer, but didn't register copyright on the name.

7 Czech Hippies Painted the John Lennon Wall
The image of Lennon was the post-Communist work of a Mexican art student *(see p81)*.

8 Absinth Will Make You Crazy
The amount of wormwood in the drink is negligible.

9 Czechs and Slovaks are the Same Nation
Despite claims that they form a single nation, the languages and mentalities are different.

10 Prague is the New Left Bank
After the Revolution, some wag proclaimed Prague "the Paris of the '90s", due to the number of free-loading expats.

Left **Mirror Maze entrance** Right **Gargoyle, St Vitus's Cathedral**

🔟 Children's Attractions

Mirror Maze
1 The warped mirrors lining the walls here are great fun for making faces, pointing fingers at distended bellies and elongated bodies and giggling hysterically, whatever your age. For older children interested in a bit of gore and history combined, the battle-scene diorama is another of the many attractions on Petřín Hill *(see pp32–3)*.

Swan Feeding
2 Grab a bag of breadcrumbs and head to the riverbank. Střelecký Ostrov is an ideal spot to watch these graceful white birds dip their necks in the water to catch the morsels for children's delight. Take care that little feet don't go into the water and mud, however, and make sure that fingers don't inadvertently get snapped in the feeding frenzy. Good for all seasons.
🅢 *Map D4*

Czech puppets

Puppet Shows
3 Puppetry is a long-standing Czech tradition, and late afternoon shows will keep kids entertained for up to an hour. There's enough action that younger folk usually don't mind not understanding the libretto or narration. Weekend presentations of well-known fairy tales at the National Marionette Theatre can fill up quickly, so book in advance *(see p65)*.

Gargoyle-Spotting
4 It's habit-forming. Give the little ones their first taste finding faces on St Vitus's Cathedral *(see pp12–13)* and they'll have their heads pointed upwards for days. In addition to gargoyles, train your kids to spot the innumerable statues, house signs *(see pp42–3)* and strange faces that adorn arches, cornices and gateways all over the city. Just take care that they don't get stiff necks or stumble on uneven pavement surfaces.

White Tower
5 This is an entertaining spot at Prague Castle. Here they can shoot a real crossbow, pick out their favourite suit of armour and imagine the grisly goings-on in the torture chamber. Little people will have no trouble negotiating the low, narrow passages, but adults might. 🅢 *Zlatá ulička, Prague Castle • Map C2 • Open Apr–Oct: 9am–5pm, Nov–Mar: 9am–4pm • Adm*

Boat on the Vltava

Historic Tram No. 91

The old-fashioned streetcar runs a circuit around the city in about 30 minutes. A friendly conductor will take your Kč35 fare and you can hop on and off at any stop on the route, including Malostranská and Národní divadlo *(see p64)*. Very handy when you can't face walking another step. For those who are planning ahead, the end station is Výstaviště, scene of more excitement. § *Map B5 • Apr–Nov: noon–5pm Sat & Sun • www.dpp.cz*

Výstaviště

In addition to Křižík Fountain, the Prague exhibition grounds are home to the Lunapark carnival: ferris wheels, rollercoasters and other similar rides will toss and turn the kids for hours, and, if they can still stomach it, there's even candy floss (cotton candy). The fun begins in March and carries on through the warmer summer months *(see p116)*.

Boat Trips

While adults might enjoy the old-fashioned (and more romantic) rowboats, children prefer the splashing, pedalling action of the miniature paddleboats that travel up and down the Vltava. Numerous vendors rent boats and sell tickets in the vicinity of Charles Bridge *(see pp18–19)*. Take all the usual precautions that no one goes overboard, accidentally or otherwise.

Black Light Theatre

There is an abundance of Black Light shows around the Old Town *(see p64)*, but the best is at Divadlo Ta Fantastika. So long as the kids don't mind strange images suddenly popping out of the dark, the brilliant displays should keep them mesmerized. § *Divadlo Ta Fantastika, Karlova 8 • Map K4*

Prague Zoo

Located on a rocky slope overlooking the right bank of river Vltava, the Prague Zoo covers an area of 64 hectares (160 acres). It was founded in 1924, and is home to 2,500 animals representing 500 species, 50 of them extremely rare in the wild • *U Trojského zámku 120, Troja • Map B5 • 296 112230*

Lunapark Carnival, Výstaviště

Left **Artěl** Right **Hračky**

ᵀᴼᴾ10 Shops and Markets

1 Dr Stuart's Botanicus

Here you'll find oils and salts for that hot bath your travel-weary feet crave, as well as perfumes, candles, soaps and every natural health and beauty product you can imagine. Branches are scattered around town but the main one is off the Old Town Square (see p76).

2 Artěl

Named after a group of Bohemian artisans established in the early 1900s, Artěl has taken the time-honoured art of glassmaking and, working hand in hand with highly skilled craftspeople, has created a collection of fresh, whimsical yet elegant designs. ✆ Celetná 29 (entrance from Rybná) • Map N3

3 Havelský trh

The Old Town's largest outdoor market. Monday through Friday the stalls in front of St Havel are crowded with produce as well as handicrafts and textiles. The greengrocers stay away at weekends, leaving more room for souvenirs. ✆ Havelský trh • Map M5

Dr Stuart's Botanicus

Art Deco

4 Art Deco

Enter this shop filled with antique furnishings, vintage clothing and one-of-a-kind knick-knacks and you'll feel you've stepped back into the First Republic. Outfit yourself in Jazz-Age style, right down to the spats and cigarette holder, or dress up your parlour with an Art Nouveau clock or cordial set. ✆ Michalská 21 • Map L5

5 Cat's Gallery (Kočičí galerie)

This delightful little shop in Týnská Street has vast collections of mugs, magnets, pictures, paintings, sculptures and other items that all have one thing in common – they depict cats in one form or another. This is a must-see for cat lovers and a great place to buy cat motif souvenirs and mementos. ✆ Týnská 9 • Map M3

6 Czech Ceramics (Česká Keramika)

While walking through the "souvenir" Karlova Street, set aside the time to stop at this

small shop, where every item on display is a testimony to Czech traditional arts and crafts.
◈ Karlova 3 • Map K4

Dorotheum

Dorotheum offices throughout the world trace their roots back to the Vienna pawnbroking office, established by Emperor Josef I in 1707. A member of the Association of International Auctioneers, Dorotheum holds large auctions several times a year and maintains a large sales gallery of paintings, silverware, fine china, jewellery, glassware and other collectors' items. ◈ Ovocný trh 2 • Map N4

Blue

Forget the traditional image of dust-collecting glass bowls and stemware. Blue's bold and quirky designs will brighten your living room, dining room or bathroom like no old-fashioned glass can. Plus, the prices are low enough that you won't hesitate to use your purchases every day. You can also pick up the requisite T-shirts, picture books and other gifts here if you wish (see p76).

Blue

Hračky

This small shop is crammed full with hundreds of charming toys. Traditional, hand-painted folk dolls, wind up toys, construction sets and model trains are just some of the goods on offer. Take advantage of the reasonable prices which are lower than elsewhere in Prague. ◈ Loretánské náměstí 3 • Map A2

Erpet Bohemia Crystal

A one-stop shop for glass and jewellery. Erpet sells Bohemian lead crystal, garnet jewellery, enamel glass and chandeliers, as well as fine goods from the Moser, Goebel and Swarovski manufacturers. Shoppers can ponder the purchases they're about to make over coffee in the shop's comfortable lounge area.
◈ Staroměstské náměstí 27 • Map M3

Left **Potato knedlíky with sauerkraut** Centre **Rohlíky** Right **Liver knedlíky in beef broth**

🔟 Prague Dishes

1 Guláš
Not quite as spicy as its Hungarian cousin, Czech goulash is essentially a rich beef stew minus the vegetables. Don't even think of ordering it without *knedlíky* dumplings on the side. Beef is the standard recipe of this staple dish, but you can sometimes find goulash using venison, chicken and even vegetarian variants.

2 Svíčková na smetaně
This is goulash's sweet cousin: slices of pot-roasted beef tenderloin are served in a carrot-sweetened cream sauce, topped with a dollop of whipped cream and cranberries. Apparently, this is one of President Václav Havel's favourite dishes. Like goulash, it's unthinkable to eat it without the dumplings to mop up the sauce.

3 Smažený sýr
Comparable to fried mozzarella sticks, this battered block of deep-fried mild cheese is usually served with French fries *(hranolky)* and a tangy tartare sauce. As with much of Czech cuisine, try not to think about the cholesterol.

4 Utopence
These pickled sausages, slightly sour, fatty and always piled high with pickled onions, are an ideal accompaniment to the local beer, as a lunchtime or early evening snack.

5 Knedlíky
These doughy dumplings are the side dish of choice for many gravy-laden Czech dishes. In addition to the savoury varieties, made with bread, potato or bacon *(špekové)*, *knedlíky* also come stuffed with fruit *(ovocné knedlíky)*, the most popular variety being plums *(švestkové)*.

6 Pivní sýr
"Beer cheese" is marinated in ale until semi-soft. It is best enjoyed spread on dark sourdough bread and sprinkled with chopped onions.

7 Syrečky
Also known as *olomoucké tvarůžky*, these small cheese rounds immediately announce themselves by their pungent aroma. Eat them as a snack or light lunch, accompanied by beer, bread and onions.

Svíčková na smetaně

Ovocné knedlíky

8 Vepřoknedlozelo

This name is the shortened version for *vepřové, knedlíky a zelí* – pork, dumplings and sauerkraut. Heavy on fat and low on flavour, this is true Czech soul food. Order it instead of goulash and you'll impress your waiter with how acclimatized you are, assuming you pronounce it right, of course.

9 Halušky

The Germans call these coarse little noodles *Spaetzle*. They're included in the Czech culinary canon as a nod to nearby Slovakia, from which they originate and with whom Bohemia has shared so much history. You can either order them *s zelím* (with sauerkraut) or *s bryndzou* (with a creamy, sharp cheese). The dish is a filling and cheap Eastern European alternative to pasta.

10 Rohlíky

The work-horse of the Prague diet, these ubiquitous banana-shaped bread rolls are served up to accompany the main meal at breakfast, lunch and dinner. Dip them in soft cheese or your dish's sauce, spread them with pâté or order them hot-dog style on nearly every street corner.

Top 10 Czech Beers

1 Staropramen
The home-town favourite has a light, fruity flavour. Brewed in the Smíchov district, its popularity owes as much to marketing as it does to local pride.

2 Pilsner Urquell
The best-known Czech beer on the international market comes from the town of Plzeň, 80 km (50 miles) southwest of Prague. It has a strong, hoppy flavour.

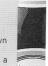

3 Krušovice
Rudolph II established the Krušovice brewery, which produces this sweet and somewhat flat beer. Try the syrupy dark *(tmavé)* variety.

4 Budvar
Brewed in the town of České Budějovice, the beer is no relation to the American Budweiser *(see p53)*.

5 Velkopopovický Kozel
This strong, smooth beer is well worth seeking out – some consider it the world's finest.

6 Velvet
This sophisticated stout, brewed by Staropramen, is catching on in Prague.

7 Gambrinus
Brewed by Pilsner Urquell, this is the best-selling beer in the country. Try the 11° variety.

8 Bernard
This unpasteurized beer has a distinct, bitter-sweet flavour and a hoppy aroma.

9 Herold
Here's a twist: Americans brewing beer in Bohemia. The centuries-old recipe produces a caramel, malty brew.

10 Braník
Braník is made with real Vltava river water, giving it its distinct flavour.

Left **Pivovarský dům** Right **U Zlatého tygra**

Bars and Kavárnas

Café Slavia

U Fleků

The city's oldest brewing pub, U Fleků is famous for its delicious, dark lager and somewhat more than modest prices. Despite what anyone tells you, the Becherovka shots are not complimentary and the rounds keep coming until you say *"ne"* five times. Very popular with busloads of tourists, and not without reason *(see p112)*.

Pivovarský dům

Excellent, rustic Czech fare served in a genteel setting. The house brewmaster is always concocting strange new flavours for his drinks, such as coffee lager or champagne ale. You can also watch the fermenting vats that will eventually become beer, if the process of brewing interests you. ◈ *Lípová 15 • Map F6 • 296 216666 • Dis. access •* **KK**

Café Slavia

Across from the National Theatre and on a busy river thoroughfare, Café Slavia with its 1930s Art Deco interior is a famous literary café. Enjoy a coffee and dessert at the end of the day or after a night at the theatre admiring the view of the riverside and Prague Castle. ◈ *Národní třída 1 • Map J6 • 224 218493 •* **KKK**

U Zlatého tygra

This legendary pub, famed as the haunt of the late writer Bohumíl Hrabal *(see p45)*, serves the finest mug of Pilsner Urquell in the city. Regulars were nonplussed when President Václav Havel brought former US president Bill Clinton in for a cold glass, so don't expect them to take much interest in you. If you find a seat, it probably means one of the regulars has died. ◈ *Husova 17 • Map L4 • 222 221111 • No credit cards •* **K**

Tretter's

This is Prague's – and perhaps Europe's – best cocktail bar. It may look like a Jazz-Age time capsule, but Tretter's is actually a relative newcomer, and highly welcome at that. You'll find no bottle juggling,

Tretter's

➤ Kavárna *is the Czech name for a Prague coffeehouse.*

O'Che's

just serious mixology, very dry martinis and, if you're lucky, a seat. Open until 3am. ◉ *V Kolkovně 3 • Map L2 • 224 811165*

Bugsy's

The kind of bar where you'll find well-heeled septugenarian gents with a girl on either arm. With top-notch drinks, sit at the bar for the best service but look smart as the under-dressed are turned away. ◉ *Pařížská 10 • Map L2 • 840 284797 • www.bugsybar.com*

Grand Café Orient

This café was designed during the Cubist movement in 1912 by Josef Gočár. Patrons will love the building's architecture and be fascinated by the tower of cakes that greets them at the entrance. The café serves everything from tea, breakfast and lunch menus, as well as wine and cocktails. ◉ *Ovocný trh 19 • Map N4 • 224 224240 •* **KK**

Black Angel's

This bar, located in the second basement of hotel U Prince, boasts 1930s-style decor. In 2012, it was listed as one of the top 50 bars of the world by *The Sunday Times*. Sip on the excellent cocktails while enjoying fabulous views of the Old Town Square and City Centre. ◉ *Staroměstské náměstí 29 • Map L4 • 224 213807 • www.blackangelsbar.cz*

O'Che's

An improbable combination of Irish and Cuban themes actually works a treat, with Sunday roasts and Guinness on tap. When the football's on, expect the bar to be filled with a hooligan-free crowd of locals, tourists and expatriates. Unfortunately, the fun stops at midnight. ◉ *Liliová 14 • Map K5 • 222 221178 • www.oches.com •* **KK**

Chapeau Rouge

The bar next to the Church of St James *(see p74)* has lost some, but not all, of the seediness that characterized its previous incarnation, where the motto was "the customer is always wrong". Backpackers still chat each other up over absinth, however, and men in the street will offer you hashish on your way in. It may sound unappealing, but it's a true Prague experience. ◉ *Jakubská 2 • Map N3 • 222 316328*

Left **Alcron** Right **Kampa Park**

Restaurants

Kampa Park
Consistently rated Prague's best restaurant, chic Kampa Park has an unparalleled riverside location and an outstanding menu with influences from all over the world *(see p89)*. Part of the Kampa Group, which has another excellent restaurant in the city.

La Degustation (Bohême Bourgeoise)
One of the most intriguing dining experiences in Prague, with chefs offering a choice of three seven-course taster menus that unfold over a three-hour period. The restaurant won a Michelin star in 2012. ◎ *Haštalská 18 • Map N2 • 222 311234 • Dis. access • KKKKK*

La Finestra in Cucina
Traditional and delicious Italian cuisine is served in a delightfully cosy setting. There is an open kitchen that allows diners to watch the chef as he prepares their meal, and an impressive selection of French wines. ◎ *Platnéřská 13 • Map K4 • 222 325325 • Dis. access • KKKKK*

Pálffy Palác

V Zátiší

V Zátiší
Prague was introduced to fine dining at this small Bethlehem Square restaurant. The *dégustation* menu – a selection of tasters – brings out the kitchen's best and pairs it with select Moravian wines. The seafood is so good you'll forget you're in a landlocked country. ◎ *Liliová 1 • Map K5 • 222 221155 • Dis. access • KKKKK*

Terasa U Zlaté Studně
Dining atop the hotel of the same name *(see p138)*, guests "At the Golden Well" may think they've died and gone to heaven. The classic Continental cuisine matches the view – but only just. The dining room is tiny, so be sure to make a reservation. ◎ *U Zlaté Studně 4 • Map C2 • 257 533322 • KKKKK*

Alcron
Seafood is the speciality at the restaurant of the Radisson *(see p139)*, but the chef is happy to prepare almost any dish. Just ask him as he makes the rounds of this minute Art Deco lounge. If the dining room is full, try

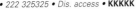

For a guide to price ranges **See p79**

La Rotonde across the foyer. After dinner, you can enjoy cocktails and live jazz in the Be Bop bar. ⊗ *Štěpánská 40* • *222 820410* • *Dis. access* • **KKKKK**

Pálffy Palác
7 Enjoy the romantic ambience in one of the most famous Baroque buildings in town. Nestled in one of Prague Castle's imposing walls, this fine dining establishment offers something special with palatial surroundings and an expansive, ever-changing menu of traditional Czech and European cuisine. A memorable dining experience with impeccable service. If you can't secure a table, choose a takeaway dish from the Pálffy Delicatessen menu *(see p89)*.

Terasa U Zlaté Studně

Plzeňská restaurace v Obecním domu
8 It may be a bit touristy, but nevertheless, gorgeous tiled mosaics of bucolic Bohemians cover the walls while an accordionist rolls out the Beer-Barrel Polka almost non-stop. The traditional food and beer are quite good and fairly priced. ⊗ *Náměstí Republiky 5* • *Map P3* • *222 002770* • *Dis. access* • **KKKK**

Cotto Crudo
9 The Four Seasons' restaurant is the toast of the town even with other top restaurateurs. Expect highly attentive service and stylish, authentic Italian cuisine by Czech chef Richard Fuchs. ⊗ *Veleslavínova 2a* • *Map K3* • *221 426880* • *Dis. access* • **KKKKK**

Country Life
10 Take heart, vegetarians, you haven't been forgotten. A meat-and dairy-free lunch buffet by day, *à la carte* menu for dinner, and it's all non-smoking. Pick up organic necessities at the shop next door. ⊗ *Melantrichova 15* • *Map L4* • *224 213366* • *Dis. access* • **KK**

Left **Divadlo Alfred ve Dvoře** Right **Puppets, National Marionette Theatre**

Performing Arts Venues

Divadlo Archa

Divadlo Archa
Archa is Prague's premiere venue for avant-garde music, dance and movement theatre. Past acts have included David Byrne and France's Compagnie Pál Frenák. ✆ *Na Poříčí 26* • *Map P3*

Hybernia
After extensive reconstruction work in 2007, the Hybernia Theatre opened with the musical *Golem* by Karel Svoboda, Zdeněk Zelenka, Lou Fanánka Hagen and Philip Renč. After a year's run, 35,000 guests had attended the performances. ✆ *Hybernská 1* • *Map P4*

Divadlo Alfred ve Dvoře
A community group recently came to the financial rescue to ensure this theatre continues hosting its outstanding non-verbal theatre. ✆ *Františka Křížka 36, Holešovice* • *Map B5*

Ponec
Prague's new dance theatre has all aspects covered, from top international dance acts to workshops for young talent. ✆ *Husitská 24a, Žižkov* • *Map B6*

Divadlo Na Zábradlí
Under Communism, it was playhouses such as this that gave vent to dissident thought. By staging daring works, they helped draw world attention to events such as the outspoken young playwright Václav Havel continually getting into trouble with the law. ✆ *Anenské náměstí 5* • *Map M3*

Laterna Magika
This company was the main proponent behind black-light theatre, a genre in which black-clad actors, working against a black background, manipulate objects. See for yourself what all the fuss is about at their stage next to the National Theatre. ✆ *Národní třída 4* • *Map E4*

Národní divadlo
The National Theatre's curtain first raised for Bedřich Smetana's opera *Libuše* in 1883; you can still see this or other Czech operas on the same stage today. Go to a performance, if only to appreciate the artistic work that went into creating the theatre. ✆ *Národní třída 2* • *Map E4*

Ceiling, Národní divadlo

Auditorium, Rudolfinum

Rudolfinum
8 The Rudolfinum is home to the Czech Philharmonic. During World War II, the Nazis sought to remove Felix Mendelssohn from the gallery of statues on the roof. They inadvertently plucked Richard Wagner instead *(see p36)*. ❧ *Alšovo Nábřeží 12 • Map K2*

Stavovské divadlo
9 The Estates Theatre is well-known as the venue where Mozart's *Don Giovanni* saw its first performance. It was also the first Czech-language playhouse in what was then a largely German-speaking city. The productions occasionally leave something to be desired, but if you don't see the *Don* here, then where?
❧ *Ovocný trh 1 • Map M4*

Národní divadlo marionet
10 The National Marionette Theatre represents the pinnacle of the much-loved puppet genre, staging wonderful productions of Czech fairytales and other child-pleasing shows (in Czech). They also have the best Beatles tribute in town and a delightful marionette version of *Don Giovanni (see p54)*. ❧ *Žatecká 1 • Map L3*

Top 10 Churches for Music Recitals

1 **St Vitus's Cathedral**
Prague Castle's cathedral is a spectacular setting for classical concerts *(see pp12–13)*.

2 **St Agnes's Convent**
This medieval convent regularly holds recitals *(see pp28–9)*.

3 **Church of St Nicholas**
Hosts chamber music recitals twice daily *(see p15)*.

4 **St Nicholas's Church**
Appreciate the Malá Strana church's Baroque grandeur at a concert of sacred music *(see p82)*.

5 **Church of St James**
This active house of worship regularly invites the general public to hear its organ *(see p74)*.

6 **Mirror Chapel**
The Baroque chamber of the Clementium hosts string quartets and other small ensembles *(see p74)*.

7 **St Martin in the Wall**
Organ and other recitals are on the bill at this Gothic church, once part of the Old Town defences. ❧ *Martinská 8 • Map L6*

8 **Spanish Synagogue**
The ornate 1880 organ figures in the sacred music concerts held in this opulent synagogue *(see p101)*.

9 **St George's Basilica**
Choral and string recitals present the greatest works of Mozart, Beethoven and other composers *(see p9)*.

10 **Church of Sts Simon and Jude**
Catch an ensemble of Prague Symphony Orchestra players in this Renaissance sanctuary. ❧ *U milosrdných • Map F2*

Left **Radost FX** Right **Mecca**

🔟 Clubs

1 Radost FX

Prague's most chic disco pushes the limits with parties so hedonistic you wonder if there isn't a law against them. Hip-hop, funk and disco are the prevalent flavours on the dance floor. The vegetarian café upstairs is open until 4am. During peak lunch and dinner hours, it can be very hard to find a seat *(see p111)*.

2 Roxy

This former cinema is a must for fans of jungle and dub. Parties continue well into the morning, much to the dismay of the neighbours. Such live acts as the Asian Dub Foundation take the stage when it's not occupied by DJs or an experimental theatre production. A portion of Roxy's proceeds goes towards funding the Linhart Foundation, a non-profit organization whose aim is to promote contemporary art. Keep abreast of Roxy's events at www.roxy.cz. ◉ *Dlouhá 33* • *Map M2*

3 Palác Akropolis

In addition to being at the heart of Prague's indie and world-music scene, the Palác Akropolis hosts the likes of Ani Difranco, Apollo 440 and Transglobal Underground. The small, smoky Divadelní bar is the hippest, hosting Prague's best DJs. On the ground floor level is a café and Czech restaurant. On a more cultural note, this is also the best venue in town to hear contemporary Romany music from such local acts as Alom or Věra Bílá and Kale. ◉ *Kubelíkova 27, Žižkov* • *Map B6*

4 Karlovy lázně

The former public bathhouse, just 100 m from Charles Bridge, was converted into a dance club in the late 1990s. You can still admire the original tiles along the corridors and the splendid mosaic murals. Drained of water, the pools now serve as the dance floors. ◉ *Novotného lávka, Smetanovo nábřeží 198* • *Map J5* • *www.karlovylazne.cz*

5 SaSaZu

One of the largest entertainment facilities in Prague, capable of accommodating up to 2,500 guests, SaSaZu has welcomed many well-known performers from all around the world such as Lily Allen, Tiesto and One Republic. Awarded a

Palác Akropolis

 Radost's website at www.radostfx.cz outlines upcoming events at the club.

Karlovy lázně

Michelin Bib Gourmand, this rather hip restaurant offers excellent food from East Asia. ◎ *Bubenské nábřeží 306 • Map B5* • *www.sasazu.com*

Mecca

The proprietors of Mecca have turned this former factory in the Holešovice warehouse district into a giant dance-and-dining emporium. The food is nouvelle cuisine, the crowd trendy and the parties wonderful. A little off the beaten track – take a taxi – but the trip is worth it. The restaurant serves food until 2am. ◎ *U Průhonu 3, Holešovice* • *Map B5 • www.mecca.cz*

Jo's Garáž

A club chronicler in the mid-1990s wrote that Jo's had its finger on the pulse of Prague's "expat scene". Little has changed here since. The backpack set still bump eagerly to pop tunes on the cramped cellar dance floor. If you're hungry, upstairs is a restaurant serving passable Tex-Mex food. ◎ *Malostranské náměstí 7 • Map C2*

U Malého Glena

The shoebox-sized cellar at "Little Glenn's" has to be Prague's smallest jazz venue. The music ranges from African-inspired drumming to blues to modern jazz, and most of it is of a high standard. Upstairs is a café where you can get

reasonable food and brunch at weekends. From the same entrepreneurs who brought you Bohemia Bagels *(see p88)*. ◎ *Karmelitská 23 • Map C3*

Rock Café

Prague's music scene is teeming with so-called "revival bands", most of whom take the stage here and entertain audiences with tributes to everyone from Jimi Hendrix to Sadé. There are also several bars, an Internet café and a screening room where you can watch films of various past rock concerts. ◎ *Národní 20 • Map L6*

Lucerna

Local "big-beat" acts are the mainstay at this Wenceslas Square music bar, but it occasionally hosts big names in jazz such as Maceo Parker, as well as where-are-they-now relics. (A separate adjoining venue, the Velký sál, or large hall, hosts bigger acts such as Wynton Marsalis.) The club's 1980s and 1990s night is one of the biggest dance parties in town. ◎ *Vodičkova 36 • Map F4*

U Malého Glena

Left **Karlovy Vary International Film Festival** Right **Prague Spring International Music Festival**

🔟 Festivals

1 Prague Spring International Music Festival

Bedřich Smetana's *Má vlast (My Country)* kicks off the annual three-week festival that draws classical music performers and fans from around the globe. The round of concerts closes with Beethoven's Ninth symphony.
🅢 May–Jun

2 Bohemia International Folklore Dance Festival

This festival has been a success since its first staging in 2005. It has now expanded beyond Prague, as DanceBohemia, and brings amateur folklore dance ensembles together from all around the world. 🅢 Aug

3 Karlovy Vary International Film Festival

It's easier to hobnob with the stars here than at Cannes or Berlin. Hundreds of partygoers turn the sleepy west Bohemian spa town upside down for nine days. Hundreds of screenings, too. 🅢 Jul

4 May Day

The dawn finds young lovers dragging themselves home after a night of doing what comes naturally on Petřín Hill *(see pp32–3)*. While they sleep, their parents spend the national holiday trying to forget the old obligatory Communist rallies.
🅢 1 May

Street Theatre Festival

5 Street Theatre Festival

Za dveřmi (Behind the Door) is an international street art festival that presents drama, acrobatics, parades and juggling on the streets and squares of Prague. 🅢 Jul

6 Tanec Praha

This international dance festival is on the verge of becoming something great. The local dance scene has greatly benefited from it, and audiences can now see contemporary productions year-round. 🅢 May, Jun

7 Pardubice Steeplechase

With 31 jumps stretching over 7 km (4 miles), this is one of the biggest steeple-chases in Europe. The first steeplechase here was held in 1874. 🅢 Oct

8 Prague Writer's Festival
Salman Rushdie, Susan Sontag and Elie Wiesel are just some of the internationally acclaimed authors who have attended this annual event. The organizers often get grief for giving Czech writers short shrift. ◈ *Time varies every year*

9 Masopust
Czech swine start getting nervous in early February as the nation whets its appetite and knives for their version of Carnival. While the beer-and-pork orgies are more common in villages than in the big city, working-class Žižkov *(see p116)* throws a large party each year. ◈ *Shrove Tue*

10 Mikuláš, Vánoce, Silvestr
Czech Christmas celebrations are largely devoid of religion, but the mulled wine starts flowing on St Nicholas's Day and doesn't stop until the Christmas carp is all eaten and New Year's Eve *(Silvestr)* fireworks arsenals are depleted. ◈ *Dec*

Christmas, Old Town Square

Top 10 National Holidays

1 Renewal of Independent Czech State
Marks the split of Czechoslovakia in 1993. ◈ *1 Jan*

2 Easter Monday
Men give their women a gentle whipping with a willow switch. Ladies respond with eggs. ◈ *Mar–Apr*

3 Labour Day
Romantics lay flowers before the statue of Karel Hynech Mácha on Petřín Hill. ◈ *1 May*

4 Day of Liberation
Plaques around town are adorned with flowers to remember those killed by the Germans in 1945. ◈ *8 May*

5 Cyril and Methodius Day
The Greek missionaries brought both Christianity and the Cyrillic alphabet to the Slavs *(see p39)*. ◈ *5 Jul*

6 Jan Hus Day
Czechs head for the hills where they roast sausages *(see p35)*. ◈ *6 Jul*

7 Czech Statehood Day
On St Wenceslas Day, as most Czechs call it, Bohemia's history is recalled. ◈ *28 Sep*

8 Independence Day
On this date in 1918 Czechoslovakia declared itself independent of Austro-Hungary. ◈ *28 Oct*

9 Day of the Fight for Freedom and Democracy
The anniversary of the 1989 Velvet Revolution. Candles and flowers are placed in various locations. ◈ *17 Nov*

10 Christmas
Streets fill with carp sellers and hedonists drinking mulled wine. ◈ *24–26 Dec*

AROUND TOWN

PRAGUE'S TOP 10

Left **House sign, Celetná** Centre **U Rotta, Malé Námestí** Right **Clock, Old Town Hall**

Old Town

PRAGUE'S HEART IS A LAYERED CAKE OF HISTORY: *its oldest buildings have double cellars, owing to a flood-prevention programme that buried the original streets 3 m (10 ft) beneath those existing today; architecturally, it embraces every epoch from Romanesque to the Brutalist style of the Kotva department store. Historically, the burghers of the Old Town (Staré Město) were ill at ease with the castle, and vice versa, the town being a bastion of Protestant feistiness, and Old Town is still livelier than Hradčany – its cafés, clubs, restaurants and theatres keep the district buzzing around the clock.*

🔟 Sights

1. Old Town Square
2. Municipal House
3. Powder Gate
4. Celetná
5. Church of St James
6. Ungelt
7. Clementinum
8. Karlova
9. Church of St Nicholas
10. Bethlehem Square

Mosaic, Municipal House

1 Old Town Square

Over the centuries, this now placid square at the heart of the city has witnessed hundreds of executions, political capitulations and, more recently of course, riotous ice hockey celebrations, a sport about which Czechs are fanatical. Today, the action is more likely to come from the crowds of tourists and Praguers, enjoying a coffee or a beer at one of the numerous pavement cafés. Dominated by the splendid Church of Our Lady before Týn, the square is always buzzing; in winter and summer, it's a wonderful place to watch the world go by *(see pp14–17)*.

Church of Our Lady before Týn, Old Town Square

2 Municipal House

National Revival artist Alfons Mucha was one of many to lend his talents to the Municipal House *(Obecní Dům)*, Prague's star Art Nouveau attraction. One of its most beautiful and striking features is Karel Špillar's mosaic above the main entrance, entitled *Homage to Prague*. It also has a firm place in history as it was from the Municipal House that Czechoslovakia was declared an independent state in 1918. Today, it is home to restaurants, cafés, exhibition halls, shops and the Prague Symphony Orchestra.
Ⓢ *Náměstí Republiky 5 • Map P3 • 222 002101 for tours • Adm • Dis. access*

3 Powder Gate

In the 15th century, King Vladislav II laid the cornerstone for this tower at the city's eastern gate, intended to complement the Royal Court nearby. Used to store gunpowder in the 17th century, hence the name, the tower was damaged during attacks by Prussian forces in 1757. The Neo-Gothic façade seen today, with its sculptural decoration, dates from 1876.
Ⓢ *Náměstí Republiky • Map P4 • Open Apr–Sep: 10am–10pm; Oct, Mar: 10am–8pm; Nov–Feb: 10am–6pm • Adm*

Powder Gate

Plaque, Clementium

Celetná
The medieval route from the silver-mining town of Kutná Hora in Bohemia passed down the street known today as Celetná, through Old Town Square and on to Prague Castle. There's still a lot of traffic on the gently curving street. ◈ Map N4

Church of St James
The Gothic and Baroque interior here wins the award for Prague's creepiest sanctuary. The church is best known for

Pietà carving, Church of St James

the legend of the mummified arm hanging above the door (see p52), but visitors should not miss the opportunity to take in one of the organ recitals held here (see p65). ◈ Malá Štupartská 6 • Map N3 • Open 9:30am–noon & 2–4pm daily (except during Mass) • Free • Dis. access

Ungelt
Also known as Týn Courtyard, this was a fortified merchants settlement in the 10th century. The Baroque and Renaissance houses were completely renovated in the early 1990s, creating what is now one of the Old Town's most charming mercantile centres. ◈ Map M3

Clementinum
Built as a Jesuit college in the mid-17th century, the Clementinum now houses the National Library. Astronomer Johannes Kepler (see p35) discovered the laws of planetary motion atop the Astronomical Tower. The Mirror Chapel hosts various concerts. ◈ Křížovnická 190, Mariánské náměstí 5 & Karlova 1 • Map K4 • 222 220879 • Library, Mirror Chapel, Astronomical Tower: Open 10am–4pm daily (Apr–Oct: to 5pm); concerts from 5pm daily (Apr–Oct: from 6pm) • Adm • Dis. access

Karlova

8 You will inevitably get lost trying to follow "Charles Street" from Old Town Square to Charles Bridge; relax and enjoy the bewildering, twisting alleys choked with shops and cafés. ✎ *Map K4*

Church of St Nicholas

9 This Baroque jewel started life as a parish church. During World War II, it was used as a garrison for Czech troops. It now belongs to the Hussite Church and also operates as a concert hall. ✎ *Staroměstské náměstí • Map L3 • Open 10am–4pm daily • Adm for masses and concerts*

Bethlehem Square

10 The 15th-century Catholic reformer Jan Hus *(see p35)* preached in the reconstructed chapel on the square's north side. The original church was converted into apartments in the 18th century but had a loving restoration to its former state in the 1950s. ✎ *Map K5 • Chapel: Open Apr–Oct: 10am–6:30pm daily; Nov–Mar: 10am–5:30pm Tue–Sun • Adm*

Bethlehem Chapel, Bethlehem Square

Around Town – Old Town

A Stroll Around the Old Town

Morning

⏰ After breakfast at the **Municipal House** café *(see p73)*, take a guided tour of the building, then go and climb the **Powder Gate** *(see p73)* for the views next door before the caffeine wears off.

Wander down **Celetná**, ducking through the arcade to Štupartská and the **Church of St James**. If you have at least 45 minutes before the top of the hour, tour the **Old Town Hall** and watch the Apostles' show on the Astronomical Clock from backstage *(see pp16–17)*. Otherwise, shop in the **Ungelt** and join the crowd below the clock outside to see the spectacle.

🍴 For lunch, head to the **Kogo** restaurant *(see p79)* for some delicious contemporary food.

Afternoon

Circumnavigate **Old Town Square** *(see pp14–15)* before entering the meandering turns of **Karlova** and wandering leisurely past the area's old buildings to **Bethlehem Square**. Have a tour of the lovely Bethlehem Chapel, then find your way back to Karlova to visit the **Clementinum**.

☕ Alternatively, if you're now a little on the tired side, have a coffee at **Café de Paris** *(see p78)* before freshening up for dinner. If you're heading to the theatre or a concert, curtains go up around 7:30pm, so it is sensible to dine afterwards.

Left **Blue** Right **Dr Stuart's Botanicus**

🔟 Shops

1 Blue
A dazzlingly different kind of glass shop. Modern, fun designs in bowls and other knick-knacks, as well as T-shirts and other tourist fare *(see p57)*. ◈ *Malé náměstí 14 • Map L4*

2 Moser
Classic crystal and cut glass produced by this well-known manufacturer. Even if you're not interested in a large vase or a crystal hedgehog, it's worth a look around. ◈ *Staroměstské náměstí 15 • Map L4*

3 Charles University Gift Shop
Looking for cool souvenirs to take back for the kids? Problem solved: a Charles University pullover. If it's chilly out, you'll want one for yourself as well. ◈ *Celetná 14 • Map M3*

4 Franz Kafka Bookshop
Here you can find a wide range of Czech literature in translation, coffee-table books and catalogues from recent exhibitions next door at the Municipal Gallery, plus classical music CDs. ◈ *Staroměstské náměstí 12 • Map M3*

5 Herbs Shop Grešík
A variety of Czech herbs, spices, tea or drops, ointments, baths, medicinal herbs and food supplements can be found in this lovely shop. ◈ *Jilská 1 • Map L5*

6 Dr Stuart's Botanicus
The store's all-natural health and beauty products are produced at a "historic village" east of Prague; enquire about tours. Herbs, oils and other seasonings, too *(see p56)*. ◈ *Týn 3 • Map M3*

7 Galerie Ztichlá klika bookshop
The name of the gallery, which translates as "silenced doorhandle" originated in a pub in the Slovak city of Košice after two days of drinking and mulling over a name for a Košice-Praha samizdat magazine. The owner, Jan Placak, loved it so much he had it patented for his bookshop. ◈ *Betlémská 10–14 • Map K5*

8 Czech Folk Crafts (Manufaktura)
Kids these days might not appreciate the handmade wooden toys or corn-husk dolls, but when was the last time you bought yourself a gift? ◈ *Karlova 26 • Map L4*

9 Český Porcelán
Bohemian porcelain might not be as prestigious as Bohemian crystal, but it makes a good souvenir. ◈ *Perlová 1 • Map L5*

10 Keramika
Probably every Czech kitchen has at least one of these ceramic plates. The traditional folk patterns are blue, red or yellow. ◈ *Havelská 21 • Map M5*

Left **Karlovy lázně** Right **Roxy**

10 Nightclubs

1 N11
Billed as Prague's first New York nightclub, N11 combines a sleek discotheque with pub-style dining. Strangely, journalists and medical staff receive a 10 per cent discount – the club's owner is both. ✆ *Národní 11 • Map E5*

2 Karlovy lázně
Bruce Willis jammed here when in town. Weekends find a queue of young clubbers stretching along the river bank waiting to get in to these remodelled municipal baths. Four levels of clubbing, from classic rock to DJs and, occasionally, live bands. ✆ *Novotného lávka • Map J5*

3 Roxy
The Old Town's most exciting club. In addition to the best dance parties in town, the former cinema hosts experimental theatre, live bands and art exhibitions. ✆ *Dlouhá 33 • Map M3*

4 Coyotes
The dance floor is not the biggest in the city, but Coyotes has a spectacular light show that puts other, bigger clubs in Prague to shame. ✆ *Malé náměstí 2 • Map L4*

5 Vagon
One of the originals for exciting live music, this place hosts blues or rock bands most nights, with a mix of well-known and unsigned acts. Always a lively atmosphere. ✆ *Národní třída 25 • Map L6*

6 Zlatý Strom
Enjoy unusual views of the Prague night sky through the glass ceilings of this subterranean club. There are two dance floors and an aquarium. ✆ *Karlova 6 • Map K4*

7 Klub Lávka
Atmospherically located right by Charles Bridge, this discobar is open 24 hours a day. In summer, you can enjoy the terrace and garden restaurant, and even rent a boat. ✆ *Novotného lávka 1 • Map J5*

8 Friends
The name fits. Prague's best gay cocktail bar has a steady following among expat and local men who are less interested in cruising than in just having a drink with like-minded folks. The owner Michael will tell you what's what. ✆ *Bartolomějská 11 • Map K6*

9 AghaRTA Jazz Centrum
Named after Miles Davis's important album from the 1970s and opened the day following his death, this club features daily performances by top Czech musicians. The AghaRTA Prague Jazz Festival is hosted annually by the club. ✆ *Železná 16 • Map M4*

10 Jazz Club U Staré paní
Prague's favourite jazz club may not look like much from the outside, but the best local acts perform here regularly to full houses. Relatively high cover charges can't keep fans away. ✆ *Michalská 9 • Map L5*

Left **Café Obecní dům** Right **Café de Paris**

Cafés and Pubs

Café Obecní dům
Dressed to the nines in Art Nouveau splendour, the Municipal House café glitters. Stop in for breakfast. ® *Náměstí Republiky 5 • Map P3*

Café de Paris
If you're not already staying at the Hotel Paříž, you may be tempted to take a room just so you can have your morning coffee in this Jugendstil café. Superior service. ® *Hotel Paříž, U Obecního domu 1 • Map P3*

Le Patio
A sushi bar heightens the trendy feeling at this "world-beat" café. There is an extensive dinner menu with classic French dishes as well as Czech specialities. Open for breakfast and lunch, with live bands in the evenings. ® *Národní třída 22 • Map L6 • 274 810262 • Dis. access* • **KKK**

Ebel Coffeehouse
You won't find a better cup of coffee in the city than at Ebel, which uses beans from all over the world. A stone's throw from Old Town Square. ® *Řetezová 9 • Map L5*

Týnská Literární kavárna
The local customers here are serious about their literature, at this café attached to a bookstore. The hidden courtyard is a blissfully quiet space to enjoy a beer on summer nights. ® *Týnská 6 • Map M3*

Grand Café Praha
Unlike other establishments on the square, this coffee house actually offers great value and good service. ® *Staroměstské náměstí 22 • Map M3*

Hotel U Prince
Have an unforgettable dining experience on the rooftop terrace of Hotel U Prince. Serves as both a restaurant and café. ® *Staroměstské náměstí 29 • Map L4 • 737 261842* • **KKKK**

La Bottega di Finestra
This café caters for all tastes, with a range of Italian specialities that includes pasta dishes and vegetarian options. Breakfast is also served. ® *Platnéřská 11 • Map K4 • 222 233094 • Dis. access*

Hotel Evropa
Have traditional coffee and cakes in the heart of the city centre. ® *Václavské náměstí 25 • Map N6 • 224 215387 • Dis. access*

Atmoška (Atmosphere)
This café, pub and restaurant has ultimate views of the castle and Charles Bridge. ® *Smetanovo nábřeží 14 • Map J5* • **KK**

Discover more at **www.traveldk.com**

Above **Pasta Fresca**

Price Categories

For a three-course meal for one with half a bottle of wine (or equivalent meal), taxes and extra charges.	**K** under Kč300
	KK Kč300–Kč500
	KKK Kč500–Kč700
	KKKK Kč700–Kč1000
	KKKKK over Kč1000

🔟 Places to Eat

1 Sarah Bernhardt

French cuisine in an opulent Art Nouveau setting inspired by Alfons Mucha's paintings of the French actress. Bohumil Hrabal (see p45) celebrated the hotel in his novel *I Served the King of England*. ✆ Hotel Paříž, U Obecního domu 1 • Map P3 • 222 195900 • **KKKKK**

2 Café Imperial

A busy and popular eatery. Enjoy a seven-course menu with selected wines at the Chef's Table, which is set up in the middle of the bustling kitchen. ✆ Na Poříčí 15 • Map G2 • **KKKK**

3 Pasta Fresca

Chef Tomáš Mykytyn prepares regional Italian dishes using fresh seasonal ingredients. Three sommeliers are on hand to guide diners through the vast wine selection. ✆ Celetná 11 • Map M4 • 224 230244 • **KKKK**

4 Kogo

Serving superior Italian dishes at remarkably low prices, Kogo is wildly popular with discerning locals; book ahead. The service is marvellous. ✆ Havelská 27 • Map M5 • 224 214543 • **KKKKK**

5 Divinis

This high-end wine bar and restaurant manages to balance a modern feel with a traditional Italian atmosphere. Good quality wines complement the classic Sicilian specialities. ✆ Týnská 21 • Map M3 • 222 325440 • **KKKKK**

6 Bellevue

A gorgeous view of the castle rising above Charles Bridge, and formal, Continental dining. ✆ Smetanovo nábřeží 18 • Map J5 • 222 221443 • **KKKKK**

7 Klub architektů

Situated in a medieval cellar, this casual club specializes in "eintopf" dishes such as beef strips with sour cream and apples. ✆ Betlémské náměstí 5a • Map K5 • 602 250082 • **KKK**

8 Lehká Hlava

This vegetarian restaurant has a varied menu. It's so good you don't even notice there are no meat choices. ✆ Boršov 2 • Map K5 • 222 220665 • **KK**

9 Fish & Chips 21 Dlouha St.

This luxurious bistro offers British cuisine as well as hot dogs and burgers. ✆ Dlouhá 21 • Map M3 • 606 881414 • **KKK**

10 Staroměstská

Classic Czech dishes are served at this traditional inn. ✆ Staroměstské náměstí 19 • Map G3 • 224 213015 • Dis. access • **KKK**

Note: *Unless otherwise stated, all restaurants accept credit cards and serve vegetarian meals*

Left **House of the Two Suns, Nerudova** Right **View from Petřín Hill**

Malá Strana

MALÁ STRANA, NOW KNOWN AS THE "LITTLE QUARTER", *was originally called Prague Minor (the lesser town), a century before Charles IV moved that name across the river (see pp104–13). Floods, fires and war kept construction busy on the Vltava's left bank; few of the original Romanesque and Gothic buildings remain. During the Habsburgs' reign, grand palaces were built in Baroque style, and today many of these serve as parliament or government buildings and embassies. The area is an enclave of parks, cafés, winding streets and unassuming churches.*

Sights

1. Charles Bridge
2. Petřín Hill
3. Nerudova
4. John Lennon Wall
5. Malostranské náměstí
6. St Nicholas Church
7. Kampa Island
8. Maltézské náměstí
9. Church of Our Lady Victorious
10. Vojanovy sady

Čertovka, Kampa Island

Charles Bridge at sunset

Charles Bridge

For almost all visitors to Prague, this spectacular Gothic bridge, crossing the Vltava from the Old Town to the castle complex, remains their most memorable image of the city, long after they have returned home *(see pp18–19)*.

Petřín Hill

A more than welcome respite from the tiny, generally crowded streets in the city below is Prague's sprawling park, looking down over spires and rooftops. Enjoy the views all the way up the hill by taking the funicular train *(see pp32–3)*.

Original John Lennon Wall

Nerudova

The 19th-century Czech writer and poet Jan Neruda (1834–91) lived in the "House of the Two Suns", at the top of the street that now bears his name. Lined with former palaces, Nerudova leads uphill from Malostranské náměstí, its many winding side streets leading visitors up to Prague Castle *(see pp8–11)*. Traditionally an artists' quarter, the street is worth exploring for its many craft shops and galleries. It is also home to one of the most concentrated collections of historic house signs in the city *(see pp42–3)*. ◈ Map C2

John Lennon Wall

Prague hippies and the secret police once waged a long-running paint battle here, as the latter constantly tried to eradicate the graffiti artists' work. The original artwork, created by a Mexican student after Lennon's assassination, has been painted over many times *(see p53)*, but the so-called John Lennon Peace Club still gathers annually at this self-made shrine to sing the former Beatle's praises and songs. ◈ *Velkopřevorské náměstí* • Map D3

Malostranské náměstí

The hectic traffic that now detracts from the beauty of Malá Strana's main square seems historically fitting – in the past it has been witness to innumerable destructive fires, revolutions, including the 1618 defenestration *(see p11)*, and executions during the days when a gallows stood here. St Nicholas's Church and the adjoining Jesuit college dominate the centre of the square, while lovely Neo-Classical palace arcades and restaurants line the perimeter. One of the most important buildings is the Sněmovna palace, once the headquarters of the National Assembly, and now home to the Chamber of Deputies. ◈ *Map C2*

St Nicholas Church

St Nicholas Church

Jesuits constructed this stunning example of Baroque architecture in the early 18th century. This prominent Prague landmark was designed by the acclaimed father and son Baroque architects, Christoph and Kilian Dientzenhofer, while other prominent artists adorned the interior with exquisite carvings, statues and frescoes. From the 1950s the clock tower often served as an observation (spying) point for state security (Communist police). ◈ *Malostranské náměstí • Map C2 • Open Mar–Oct: 9am–5pm daily; Nov–Feb: 9am–4pm daily • Adm*

Kampa Island

The tiny Čertovka (Devil's Canal) that separates Kampa from Malá Strana was once the town's "laundry", milling area and, in the 17th century, home to a thriving pottery industry. A popular park now covers the island's southern end *(see p40)*, while the

Malostranské náměstí

Kampa Island

northern half is home to elegant embassies, restaurants and hotels. Much of the island was submerged during the 2002 flooding and many buildings had to be repaired. ✆ *Map D3*

Maltézské náměstí

The Knights of Malta once had an autonomous settlement here, and the square still bears their name. The area is dominated by beautiful Baroque palaces, and the 12th-century Church of Our Lady Below the Chain. The church's name refers to the chain used in the Middle Ages to close the monastery gatehouse. ✆ *Map C3*

Church of Our Lady Victorious

Also known as the Church of the Infant Jesus of Prague, Prague's first Baroque church (1611) got its name – and its Catholic outlook – after the Battle of White Mountain *(see p34)*. Visitors stream in to see the miracle-working statue of the Christ Child *(see p38)*. ✆ *Karmelitská 9 • Map C3 • Open 8:30am–7pm Mon–Sat, 8:30am–8pm Sun • Free*

Vojanovy sady

Malá Strana has many green pockets, but Vojan's gardens top them all for their romantic charm. Tulip beds, flowering fruit trees and the occasional peacock add to the fairytale atmosphere *(see p40)*. ✆ *U lužického semináře • Map D2*

A Day in Malá Strana

Morning

🕐 You can approach the Little Quarter from the Old Town as royal processions once did, by crossing **Charles Bridge** *(see pp18–19)*, or you can save your energy for the day ahead, and start from the top of the hill and walk down. Get to **Nerudova** *(see p81)* from one of the many side streets leading from Hradčany and stroll down, window shopping at the many craft outlets on your way. Don't worry if you stray off the beaten path; as long as you continue downhill, you'll end up at the area's central hub, **Malostranské náměstí**. Here, spend at least an hour savouring one of the city's most spectacular buildings, the **St Nicholas Church**.

🍴 Pause for lunch, either at one of the many cheap cafés on Malostranské náměstí or splash out at **Kampa Park** *(see p89)*.

Afternoon

After lunch, take Tomášská and Valdštejnské around to the **Wallenstein Garden** *(see p40)*. Tip-toe through the tulips at **Vojanovy sady** and continue down U lužického semináře under Charles Bridge and onto **Kampa Island**.

☕ After coffee at **Čertovka** *(see p88)*, check the writing on the **John Lennon Wall** *(see p81)* before visiting the **Church of Our Lady Victorious**.

In the evening, catch a recital at St Nicholas Church or dance the night away with the young crowd at **Jo's Garáž** *(see p67)*.

Following pages: **Kampa Island**

Left **Thun-Hohenstein Palace** Centre **Wallenstein Palace** Right **Shoenborn Palace**

Around Town – Malá Strana

TOP 10 Palaces

1 Nostitz Palace
Take in the restoration work at this 17th-century palace while enjoying a chamber music concert. The palace now serves as the seat of the Ministry of Culture. Ⓢ *Maltézské náměstí 1 • Map C3*

2 Thun-Hohenstein Palace
The Kolowrat family's heraldic eagles support the portal of this palace. Built by Giovanni Santini-Aichel in 1721, the building is now the Italian Embassy. Ⓢ *Nerudova 20 • Map C2*

3 Lichtenstein Palace
Originally several houses, Lichtenstein Palace fused in the 16th century. Today, it is home to Prague's Academy of Music and numerous concerts and recitals. Ⓢ *Malostranské náměstí 13 • Map C2*

4 Morzin Palace
The two giant Moors (hence Morzin) bearing up the Romanian Embassy's façade are said to wander about Malá Strana streets at night. Ⓢ *Nerudova 5 • Map C2*

5 Wallenstein Palace
General Wallenstein pulled out all the stops creating what is essentially a monument to himself. On the palace's frescoes, the Thirty Years' War commander had himself depicted as both Achilles and Mars. Ⓢ *Valdštejnské náměstí 4 • Map D2 • Open 10am–5pm Sat & Sun • Adm*

6 Buquoy Palace
This pink stucco palace and the John Lennon Wall are separated by only a few steps, but they are miles apart aesthetically. However, the French Ambassador helped preserve the graffiti opposite his offices in the 1980s. Ⓢ *Velkopřevorské náměstí 2 • Map D3*

7 Michna Palace
Francesco Caratti modelled this palace on Versailles. Today it's home to the Sokol Physical Culture Movement. Ⓢ *Újezd 40 • Map C4*

8 Shoenborn Palace
Count Colloredo-Mansfeld owned the palace in the 17th century: having lost a leg in the Thirty Years' War, he had the stairs reconstructed so he could ride his horse into the building. Czechoslovakia's first ambassador to the United States sold the palace to the US government in 1925. Ⓢ *Tržiště 15 • Map C3*

9 Lobkowicz Palace (Převorovských)
Home to the German Embassy; in 1989 hundreds of East Germans found their way to the West by scrambling over the embassy's back fence. Ⓢ *Vlašská 19 • Map C3*

10 Kaunitz Palace
The Yugoslav (now Serbian) Embassy sat quietly in its pink and yellow stucco for more than 300 years until war made it a popular spot for protests. Ⓢ *Mostecká 15 • Map D3*

86 *There is another Lichtenstein (also known as Kaiserstein or Odkolkovský) Palace on Kampa Island.*

Left **Clothes shop in Malá Strana** Right **V Ráji**

🔟 Shops

Beer Shop Galerie Piva
1 A large variety of bottled beers from around the country, mostly from independent producers, are sold at this store. The knowledgeable staff will helpfully guide you through the offerings available. ◈ *Lázeňská 19* • Map C3

V Ráji
2 This bookstore and publishing house specializes in foreign books on Prague. Dictionaries, calendars, postcards and other items in 21 languages are on offer. ◈ *Tomášská 10* • Map C2

U bílého jablka
3 If you can't bring yourself to leave Prague, take it with you: this shop sells adorable ceramic miniatures of the surrounding houses and other monuments. ◈ *Úvoz 1* • Map B2

Obchod vším možným
4 Just under New Castle Steps, at the end of Nerudova Street, this small shop sells original Czech puppets, gifts, toys, ceramics, jewellery, art and enamel tableware. ◈ *Nerudova 45* • Map C2

Galerie K
5 Right in the middle of Maltese Square, you will find a small shop filled with old paintings, maps and engravings of Prague. You may be surprised to see how Prague has changed over time. ◈ *Maltézské náměstí 3* • Map C3

Decastello
6 A delightful small shop offering a variety of products from jewellery and ceramics to home textiles and replicas of old weapons. ◈ *Karmelitská 26* • Map C3

Květinářství u Červeného lva
7 It appears as if a jungle is sprouting from the hole in the wall that is the "Flowershop at the Red Lion". Spruce up your apartment or hotel room with their unique arrangements. ◈ *Saská* • Map D3

Malostranské starožitnictví
8 This antiques store is a veritable treasure trove of jewellery, watches, porcelain objects, silverware, photographs and coins. It also sells larger items, such as musical instruments. ◈ *Malostranské náměstí 28* • Map C2

Absinth Shop
9 Situated under the Castle Steps in a colourful Art Nouveau building, this shop offers an assortment of Czech absinth, as well as absinth from elsewhere in Europe. Tastings are free. *Slivovitz* (plum brandy), *becherovka* liquor, wines and special cannabis beers are also on sale. ◈ *Úvoz 1* • Map C2

Vetešnictví
10 A favourite junk shop, where you can find everything from silver teaspoons to glass and door handles. ◈ *Vítězná 16* • Map C4

Left **Bohemia Bagel** Right **U zeleného čaje**

Cafés and Pubs

Bohemia Bagel
1 It's hard to believe now, but Prague had no bagels until American entrepreneurs opened this shop here in 1997, serving fresh-baked bagels, sandwiches and endless cups of coffee. Open until 7pm. *Lázeňská 19 • Map C3*

John Lennon Pub
2 This pub is all about celebrating the legendary singer. Enjoy steaks and burgers in the garden. *Hroznová 6 • Map D3*

U zeleného čaje
3 Serving imported teas, sandwiches and salads, "At the Green Tea" offers a welcome change from the ubiquitous beer and fried food. *Nerudova 19 • Map C2*

Restaurant and Beer Parlor Čertovka
4 The stairway leading to this café's riverside patio is so narrow it needs its own traffic lights. They say President Václav Havel took Pink Floyd here for beer. *U lužického semináře 24 • Map D2*

Bar Bar
5 The salads, waffles and crêpes served here make an excellent light lunch, but you'll have trouble finding a seat in the evening. *Všehrdova 17 • Map C4*

U Kocoura
6 You might think the regulars at this pub on Malá Strana's main drag would be used to tourists by now, but don't be surprised if every face turns to meet you. Serves excellent Pilsner. *Nerudova 2 • Map C2*

V Lázních
7 With its old furniture and candle lights on every table, V Lázních is made for rainy nights. Try the mulled wine. *Lázeňská 6 • Map D3*

Café Bella Vida
8 This café serves its own coffee blend and delectable mini-desserts and sandwiches. *Malostranské nábřeží 3 • Map D4*

U Hada
9 This tiny wine cellar sells excellent imported and domestic wines. If the tables out front are full, take your bottle to Petřín Hill. *Maltézské náměstí 3 • Map C3*

Café Victoria
10 Founded in 1881, this café offers tasty meals alfresco, in its sunny garden, or inside, where there is a permanent exhibition by photographer Jan Saudek. *Malostranské náměstí 38 • Map C2*

Discover more at **www.traveldk.com**

Price Categories

For a three-course meal for one with half a bottle of wine (or equivalent meal), taxes and extra charges.

K	under Kč300
KK	Kč300–Kč500
KKK	Kč500–Kč700
KKKK	Kč700–Kč1000
KKKKK	over Kč1000

Above **Cantina**

🔟 Restaurants

1 Cantina
The best Mexican food in Prague. The *fajitas* are great; try the chicken and banana variety. Book ahead. ✆ Újezd 38 • Map C4 • 257 317173 • Dis. access • **KKK**

2 Pálffy Palác
This fine-dining establishment with a view of the castle terraces seems to revel in its tattered splendour. ✆ Valdštejnská 14 • Map D2 • 257 530522 • **KKKKK**

3 Malostranská Beseda
This traditional Czech restaurant offers "forgotten" specialities such as leg of cockerel cooked in a wine-plum sauce with fried potato dumplings. ✆ Malostranské náměstí 21 • Map C2 • 257 409112 • **KK**

4 U Patrona
The Continental and Czech cuisine will please gourmets; the balcony overlooking Charles Bridge will delight romantics. ✆ Dražického náměstí 4 • Map D3 • 257 530725 • **KKKK**

5 U Maltézských rytířů
For a local treat, have the venison Chateaubriand. ✆ Prokopská 10 • Map C3 • 257 212775 • **KKKKK**

6 Kampa Park
This top riverside restaurant serves a mix of Continental classics and fusion cuisine. ✆ Na Kampě 8b • Map D3 • 257 532685 • Dis. access • **KKKKK**

7 Gitanes
A short walk from the Charles Bridge, this unpretentious restaurant serves the best of Dalmatian cuisine. ✆ Tržiště 7 • Map C3 • 257 530163 • **KKK**

8 The Little Whale (U malé velryby)
The Little Whale offers new twists on old classics in an affordable "Czech brasserie" style. With plenty of choices from calamari to steaks and the special Little Whale seafood pie. ✆ Maltézské náměstí 15 • Map C3 • 257 214703 • Dis. access • **KKKK**

9 Malostranská pivnice
Old pub-style restaurant with traditional Czech fare and excellent Pilsner beer. ✆ Cihelná 3 • Map D2 • 257 530032 • **KKK**

10 El Centro
The Spanish owners and imported chefs make sure the *paella* is just right, at this authentic and popular eatery. ✆ Maltézské náměstí 9 • Map C3 • 257 533343 • Dis. access • **KKK**

 Note: *Unless otherwise stated, all restaurants accept credit cards and serve vegetarian meals*

Left **Loreto** Right **Belvedere, Royal Garden**

Prague Castle and Hradčany

FOUNDED BY PRINCE BOŘIVOJ IN THE 9TH CENTURY, *Prague Castle and its attendant cathedral tower overlook the city from the long hill known as Hradčany. The surrounding town was founded in 1320, becoming home to servants' hovels and, after the cataclysmic fire of 1541, grand palaces. Renaissance and Baroque reconstructions in the area created much of what visitors see today. The Loreto shrine to the Virgin Mary demonstrated the growing importance of Prague to the Church. At the castle, primitive defences were removed, making room for gardens, parade grounds and the other needs of a modern empire. When the Habsburgs removed the imperial seat to Vienna, Hradčany seemed to become preserved in time, saving it from the ravages of war and modernization. The area abounds with interesting sights for art and history lovers, as well as romantic hidden lanes and parks – in short, a total expression of the Czech nation's shifting epochs and politics.*

Golden Lane

Sights

1	Prague Castle	6	Nový Svět
2	St Vitus's Cathedral	7	Sternberg Palace
3	Loreto	8	Old Castle Steps
4	Royal Garden	9	Hradčanské náměstí
5	New Castle Steps	10	Radnické schody

Discover more at **www.traveldk.com**

Prague Castle in winter

Prague Castle

1 The first and main focus of most tourists' visit to the city of Prague is the gloriously ornate and varied castle complex *(see pp8–11)*. Its determined survival in the face of an often turbulent history only seems to heighten the castle's attractiveness and fascination. Despite its medieval appearance, the castle is still as much of a political stronghold as it has always been, and currently serves as the office of the country's president, Václav Klaus.

Golden Portal, St Vitus's Cathedral

St Vitus's Cathedral

2 The Gothic splendour of St Vitus's spires can be seen from almost every vantage point in Prague, but don't miss the opportunity to see its beautiful stained-glass windows and gargoyles close up *(see pp12–13)*.

Loreto

3 The onion-domed white towers of this 17th-century church complex are like something out a fairytale, but it's up to you whether you choose to believe in the reconstruction of the Virgin Mary's house, the Santa Casa, at the heart of the building *(see pp20–21)*.

Royal Garden

4 Visitors may regret the disappearance of the maze and pineapple trees that once featured here, but are likely to appreciate the absence of Rudolph II's lions. Within the English-style garden are the former Presidential Residence (the First Lady didn't like it), the sgraffitoed Ball Game Hall and the Royal Summer Palace, also known as Belvedere. Ⓢ *U Prašného mostu • Map C1 • Open Apr–Oct: 10am–6pm daily (May & Sep: to 7pm; Jun & Jul: to 9pm; Aug: to 8pm) • Dis. access • Free*

5 New Castle Steps

The Royal Route, established in the 15th century for the coronation of George of Poděbrady, covered the distance from the Municipal House on the Náměstí Republiky *(see p73)* to the castle. The last stretch climbed the hill about here,

Nový Svět

although the original steps were reconstructed during Empress Maria Theresa's Hradčany renovation in the 18th century. Halfway up is a music pavilion, from which a brass quartet of the Castle Guard serenades the city each morning at 10am. ❧ *Map C2*

6 Nový Svět

Nestled below the Loreto *(see pp20–21)* and at the head of the Stag Moat is Nový Svět (New World), perhaps the best street in town for romantic strolling, weather permitting. The picturesque low houses were built in the 17th century to replace the medieval slums built for castle workers after the former burned down in 1541. They remain unchanged by time, still displaying their

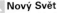

decorative house signs. Rudolph II's choleric astronomer Tycho de Brahe *(see p35)* lived at No. 1 and apparently found the noise of nearby church bells insufferable. ❧ *Map A2*

7 Sternberg Palace

This fine Baroque building, dating from 1698, houses the National Gallery's collection of European art, which is reputed to be one of the best in the country. Spread over three floors, highlights include paintings by Rubens, Rembrandt and El Greco. ❧ *Map B2*

8 Old Castle Steps

The relatively gentle slope of the Prague Castle's "back-door" entrance leads from the Malostranská metro to the castle's eastern gate. Local artists and artisans line

Old Castle Steps

Stag Moat

When the Stag Moat was not fulfilling its defensive duties, Prague's rulers used it as a hunting park. Rudolph II is said to have been particularly fond of chasing deer around the narrow, wooded gorge with his pet lions. The Powder Bridge's earthworks were excavated to permit pedestrians access to both halves of the moat.

---

the steps, selling everything from watercolour prints to polished stones. Below the steps are terraced gardens. ✆ Map D2

9 Hradčanské náměstí
Many visitors enter this square backwards, trying to fit St Vitus's spires into their viewfinders. Tear your eyes away from the castle's western face and you'll see, among other Renaissance buildings, the colourful Archbishop's Palace and the grim Schwarzenberg Palace across the way. In the green centre is a plague column from 1726; opposite the castle is the Toskánský Palace, now one of the Ministry of Foreign Affairs's buildings. ✆ Map B2

10 Radnické schody
The Courthouse Steps lead from Hradčany's former mayoral residence, now the hotel Zlatá Hvězda, to the old courthouse at Loretánská 1. At the bottom are two statues, St John of Nepomuk on the left and St Joseph with the infant Jesus in Renaissance garb on the right. There are more steps than is immediately apparent, making the pub halfway up a convenient stopping-off point. ✆ Map B2

Hradčanské náměstí

A Day in Hradčany

Morning

🕐 Start your day with a brisk climb up the **New Castle Steps**, and time your ascent to hear the 10am Castle Guard brass quartet. After a stroll through the scenic grounds, leave the castle behind and walk west through **Hradčanské náměstí**. As you pass the imposing Schwarzenberg Palace, set amid the Renaissance buildings that surround the square, take time to view some Baroque Czech art and the Old Masters collection at Sternberg Palace.

Now walk up Loretánská to Loretánské náměstí, where you'll find the vast Černín Palace staring down at the **Loreto** (see pp20–21). Explore the latter and its odd gallery of saints before lunch at **Restaurant Loreta** (see p97).

Afternoon

Exit Loretánské náměstí past the Capuchin monastery and follow Černínská downhill, pausing on **Nový Svět**. Coo over the street's piebald houses and follow Kanovnická back to Hradčanské náměstí.

The rest of the afternoon will be taken up with a tour of the unmissable **Prague Castle** (see pp8–11), **St Vitus's Cathedral** (see pp12–13), and the myriad of other attractions in the castle complex.

To end the day, find your way back to Loretánské náměstí 1 and the famed pub **U Černého vola** (see p96) for a pickled sausage and a glass of beer.

 Following pages: View of Prague and the Vltava from Hradčany

93

Left **U Černého vola** Right **Café Savoy**

Pubs and Cafés

1 U Černého vola
Part of the proceeds from the pub "At the Black Ox" go to help the nearby school for the blind. Watching the regulars knock back litre after litre of beer, you can see why. ◈ *Loretánské náměstí 1 • Map A2*

2 The Strahov Monastic Brewery
Located in the Strahov Monastery founded by King Vladislav II in 1142, this restored brewery has a capacity for 350 guests, split between the courtyard, restaurant and the brewery itself. ◈ *Strahovské nádvoří 301 • Map A2*

3 Na Baště
An out-of-the-way, peaceful café in the castle's Gardens on the Bastion, where you can rest over a cup of tea or coffee. Light snacks, too. ◈ *Zahrada na Baště, Prague Castle • Map C1*

4 Starbucks Pražský hrad
Sip an *espresso* on the rooftop while peering through one of the telescopes at the city below. The quiet patio has large tables where you can lunch and plan your visit to the castle next door. ◈ *Ke Hradu • Map C1*

5 U Labutí
"At the Swans" serves Pilsner Urquell and some substantial dishes, such as *wiener schnitzel* and goulash, on its garden terrace overlooking the upper Stag Moat. ◈ *Hradčanské náměstí 11 • Map B2*

6 Café Savoy
This café feels just like a Prague café should, with high ceilings, elegant fixtures and huge windows. Along with a standard menu, the café also has a gourmet menu and offers a selection of pastries to enjoy with a coffee. ◈ *Vítězná 5 • Map C4*

7 Café Galerie
Situated in the Sternberg Palace, this is a good spot to enjoy a cup of coffee and a baguette or a light meal after viewing the Castle and before heading off to visit the other palaces nearby. ◈ *Hradčanské náměstí 15 • Map B2*

8 Lobkowicz Palace
This pleasant and smart restaurant offers light lunches and suppers with a view of the city. The café in the courtyard is the place to end your tour of the castle. ◈ *Jiřská 3 • Map C2*

9 Café Gallery
In the narrow alleys leading into Golden Lane are a number of pavement cafés offering coffees, sandwiches, wine and spirits. Outdoor seating in good weather. ◈ *Zlatá ulička u Daliborky 42 • Map C1*

10 R+R Restaurant & Café
Visitors can escape the crowds at this café hidden in the arcade on the way to the castle. Relax with coffee and strudel, or beer and sandwiches. ◈ *Loretánská 3 • Map B2*

Above **Hradčany Restaurant**

🔟 Restaurants

1 Hradčany Restaurant
This fine-dining restaurant at the Hotel Savoy is one of the best in the country. ❧ *Keplerova 6* • *Map A2* • *224 302430* • **KKKKK**

2 Peklo
Continental dining in a grotto beneath Strahov Monastery. The house speciality, the "stuffed devil's hoof", is worth ordering. ❧ *Strahovské nadvoří 1* • *Map A3* • *220 516652* • **KKKK**

3 U Císařů (At the Emperors)
This restaurant serves traditional specialities and international favourites. The decor includes pewter tableware collections, hunting weapons and blacksmith bellows. ❧ *Loretánská 5* • *Map B2* • *220 518484* • **KKKKK**

4 Malý Buddha
The "Little Buddha" serves a wide range of potent teas and Vietnamese food. No smoking. ❧ *Úvoz 46* • *Map B2* • *220 513894* • *No credit cards* • **KK**

5 U ševce Matouše
"At the Cobbler Matouš" has made an art of melting cheese on beefsteaks. The low, vaulted room is cosy. ❧ *Loretánské náměstí 4* • *Map A2* • *220 514536* • **KKK**

6 Lví dvůr
The rooftop dining room affords incomparable views of St Vitus; the beer hall serves a sublime suckling pig. ❧ *U Prašného mostu 6* • *Map B1* • *224 372361* • **KKKKK**

7 U Zlaté hrušky
"At the Golden Pear" serves delicious Continental and Czech game dishes in picturesque Nový Svět. ❧ *Nový Svět 3* • *Map A2* • *723 764940* • **KKKKK**

8 Restaurant Loreta
A simple but reliable Czech eatery with aspirations to be something grander. Sit outdoors for a lunchtime serenade from the Loreto carillon. ❧ *Loretánské náměstí 8* • *Map A2* • *233 310510* • **KKK**

9 Host Restaurant
Excellent, stylish dining with sweeping views of Petřín Hill and Malá Strana. Accessed by a particularly steep and narrow staircase. ❧ *Loretánská 15* • *Map B2* • *728 695793* • **KKKK**

10 Villa Richter
Panoramic views of the city and the choice of two restaurants, Villa Richter has it all. While Terra offers well-priced Czech cuisine, the elegant Piano Noble serves Central European and Jewish fare. ❧ *Staré zámecké schody 6* • *Map C2* • *702 205108* • **KKKKK**

Left **Façade detail, Spanish Synagogue** Right **Vaulting, Pinkas Synagogue**

Josefov

IT IS IMPOSSIBLE TO DATE PRECISELY THE JEWS' ARRIVAL IN PRAGUE, *but historical sources mention the destruction of a Jewish settlement on the Vltava's left bank in the 13th century. For the next 500 years, Prague's Jews were obliged to live in a walled community where the Josefov quarter is today, working, studying and worshipping in the confines of the ghetto. So restricted was their allotted space that they were obliged to bury their dead layer upon layer in the Old Jewish Cemetery. When Emperor Josef II removed these strictures, many Jews left the ghetto, which became a slum occupied by the city's poorest residents. The quarter was razed in the late 19th century, making way for avenues such as Pařížská with its fine Art Nouveau houses. During World War II, the synagogues stored valuables looted from Jewish communities across the Reich – nearly 80,000 Czech and Moravian Jews perished in the Holocaust (see p25).*

🔟 Sights

1. Old Jewish Cemetery
2. Old-New Synagogue
3. St Agnes's Convent
4. Jewish Town Hall
5. High Synagogue
6. Maisel Synagogue
7. Ceremonial Hall
8. Klausen Synagogue
9. Pinkas Synagogue
10. Spanish Synagogue

Torah shield, High Synagogue

Discover more at www.traveldk.com

Old Jewish Cemetery

and chapels. The artworks here, as part of the gallery's collection, comprise some of the best Czech medieval art *(see pp28–9)*.

4 Jewish Town Hall
The hands of the town hall's Rococo clock turn backwards, as the Hebrew letters on its face are read from right to left. The building was one of Mordecai Maisel's gifts to his community in the late 16th century *(see p35)*, but it was renovated in Baroque style in 1763. ◊ *Maiselova 18 • Map L3 • Closed to the public*

1 Old Jewish Cemetery
The sight of hundreds of graves, their leaning headstones crumbling on top of each other, is a moving and unforgettable experience – a testament to the treatment of the Jews in Prague, confined to their own ghetto even in death. Although there is no definite record of the number of burial sites here, to appreciate the depth of the graveyard, compare the gravestones' height with that of the street level on U Starého hřbitova *(see pp22–3)*.

2 Old-New Synagogue
Attached to the Old Jewish Cemetery, Europe's oldest surviving synagogue has witnessed a turbulent history, including pogroms and fire, and has often been a place of refuge for the city's beleaguered Jewish community. Its name derives from the fact that another synagogue was built after this one, taking the title "new", but this was later destroyed. It is still the religious centre for Prague's small, present-day Jewish community *(see pp24–5)*.

3 St Agnes's Convent
This lovely Gothic convent, now part of the National Gallery, is full of spectacular altarpieces and wall panels, as well as original 13th-century cloisters

5 High Synagogue
Constructed along with the town hall with funds from Mordecai Maisel, the High Synagogue was built in elegant Renaissance fashion. Subsequent reconstructions updated the exterior, but the interior retains its original stucco vaults. Inside there are also impressive Torah scrolls and mantles. ◊ *Červená 2 • Map L3 • Closed to the public*

Jewish Town Hall

The Old Jewish Cemetery, Ceremonial Hall, Maisel, Pinkas, Spanish and Klausen synagogues comprise the Jewish Museum in Prague.

99

Rabbi Loew

One of Prague's most famed residents, Rabbi Loew ben Bezalel (1512–1609) is associated with numerous local legends but he was also a pioneering pedagogue and a leading Hebrew scholar of the times. Foremost among the myths surrounding Loew is that of the Golem, a clay automaton the rabbi supposedly created to defend the ghetto (see p52).

Maisel Synagogue

Rudolf II gave Mordecai Maisel permission to build his private synagogue here in the late 16th century, in gratitude for the Jewish mayor's financial help in Bohemia's war against the Turks. At the time of its construction it was the largest synagogue in Prague, until fire destroyed it and much of the ghetto in 1689. It was later rebuilt in Neo-Gothic style. Inside is a wonderful collection of Jewish silverwork and other items such as candlesticks and ceramics, much of it looted by the Nazis from other synagogues across Bohemia. Ironically, the Third

Ceremonial Hall

Reich planned to build a museum in Prague, dedicated to the Jews as an "extinct race". ⌖ Maiselova 10 • Map L3 • Open Apr–Oct: 9am–6pm Sun–Fri; Nov–Mar: 9am–4:30pm • Adm

Ceremonial Hall

Built in the early 1900s in mock Romanesque fashion, the Ceremonial Hall was home to the Jewish community's Burial Society. The exhibits inside detail the complex Jewish rituals for preparing the dead for the grave. ⌖ U Starého hřbitova 3 • Map K2 • Open Apr–Oct: 9am–6pm Sun–Fri; Nov–Mar: 9am–4:30pm • Adm

Klausen Synagogue

Abutting the Old Jewish Cemetery, this Baroque single-nave building was constructed in 1694 on the site of a school and prayer hall (klausen) where Rabbi Loew taught the cabala. Like most of the synagogues in the area, it now houses Jewish exhibitions, including prints and manuscripts. ⌖ U Starého hřbitova 1 • Map K2 • Open Apr–Oct: 9am–6pm Sun–Fri; Nov–Mar: 9am–4:30pm • Adm

Maisel Synagogue

Pinkas Synagogue

9 After World War II, this 15th-century Gothic building with some early Renaissance features became a monument to the estimated 80,000 Czech and Moravian victims of the Holocaust – the names and dates of all those known to have perished either in the Terezín concentration camp or other extermination camps across Eastern Europe are written on the wall as a moving memorial. Equally moving is the exhibition of writings and paintings made by the children (of whom there were more than 10,000 under the age of 15) confined in Terezín. ✆ *Široká 3 • Map K3 • Open Apr–Oct: 9am–6pm Sun–Fri; Nov–Mar: 9am–4:30pm • Adm*

Spanish Synagogue

10 The opulent Moorish interior with its swirling arabesques and stucco decoration gives this late 19th-century synagogue its name. It stands on the site of a building known as the Old School, Prague's first Jewish house of worship. František Škroup, composer of the Czech national anthem, was the organist here in the mid-19th century. ✆ *Vězeňská 1 • Map M2 • Open Apr–Oct: 9am–6pm Sun–Fri; Nov–Mar: 9am–4:30pm • Adm*

Alms box, Klausen Synagogue

A Day in the Jewish Quarter

Morning

🕐 A sobering place to start the day, to appreciate how large the Czech Jewish community once was, is the **Pinkas Synagogue**, where Holocaust victims are listed by their home village and name. Then take a stroll through the adjoining **Old Jewish Cemetery** *(see pp22–3)*, where a guide will help you find significant grave-sites. To lighten the mood, proceed to the **Klausen Synagogue** on the right, with its exhibits on Jewish festivals and family life.

At the end of U Starého hřbitova is the **Old-New Synagogue** *(see p99)*, where you'll find treasures like Rabbi Loew's seat. Exiting, note the **Jewish Town Hall** *(see p99)* next door with its Hebrew clock. Just a few feet away, treat yourself to lunch at **Barock** *(see p103)*.

Afternoon

After lunch, meander among the antiques shops en route to the **Maisel Synagogue**, where you'll find the first part of an exhibit on Jewish settle-ment in Bohemia and Moravia – it continues at the **Spanish Synagogue**.

Refresh yourself at **Bakeshop Praha** *(see p102)* around the corner before ending your tour at **St Agnes's Convent** *(see pp28–9)* with its exhibits of Czech medieval art.

A truly Josefov-style evening involves a kosher dinner at **King Solomon** *(see p103)* and a concert of sacred music at the **Spanish Synagogue**.

Around Town – Josefov

Left **Studio Šperk** Right **Pastries, Bakeshop Praha**

Shops

Spanish Synagogue Gift Shop

Exquisite torah pointers, *yarmulkas* (skull caps) and other unique gifts, such as a watch in the style of the clock on the Jewish Town Hall *(see p99)*. ⓢ *Vězeňská 1 • Map L2*

Knihkupectví Fišer

Famous among the student community, this bookshop is nestled within the university campus. Both the store and its owner, Fišer, featured in the Czech film *Vrchní, prchni!* ⓢ *Kaprova 10 • Map K3*

Hodinářství (Old Clocks)

If you have trouble finding this small shop selling old clocks, simply stand at the corner of Maiselova and Široká streets and you'll hear the old cuckoo clock. ⓢ *Maiselova 16 • Map L3*

Granát Turnov

Specializing in Bohemian garnet, Granát Turnov is part of Prague's biggest jewellery chain. One can find a large variety of brooches and necklaces here. ⓢ *Dlouhá 28 • Map N2*

Franz Kafka Society Bookshop

Works by Franz Kafka in German and in translation, as well as other specialized literature and books on Prague and related subjects can be found here. Guidebooks, souvenirs and gifts can also be purchased. ⓢ *Široká 14 • Map L3*

Studio Šperk

Come to this tiny goldsmith's workshop for eye-catching gold and silver jewellery, much of which is embellished with the celebrated red Bohemian garnet. ⓢ *Dlouhá 19 • Map M3*

Bakeshop Praha

Grab a bag of *rugalach*, brownies or other mouth-watering treats for on-the-go nourishment, or lunch on an egg-salad sandwich and coffee. Salads and quiches also to take away. ⓢ *Kozí 1 • Map M1*

Antique Kaprova

This serious collector's shop specializes in prints and small decorative items such as clocks and lamps. If you don't find what you're looking for, just ask and they'll point you in the right direction. ⓢ *Kaprova 12 • Map K3*

Antique Cinolter

Art lovers should peruse this small gallery's sale exhibition of local art. The original oils and sketches capture Josefov's bittersweet warmth and humanity. ⓢ *Maiselova 9 • Map L3*

Alma (Mahlerová) Antique

What don't they sell? Alma Antique is a bazaar stocked with Persian rugs, jewellery, Meissen porcelain, crystal and nesting dolls. This is one of the largest antiques dealers in Prague. ⓢ *Valentinská 7 • Map K3*

For tips on shopping in Prague See p132

Price Categories

For a three-course meal for one with half a bottle of wine (or equivalent meal), taxes and extra charges.

K	under Kč300
KK	Kč300–Kč500
KKK	Kč500–Kč700
KKKK	Kč700–Kč1000
KKKKK	over Kč1000

Above **Barock**

🔟 Cafés and Restaurants

1 Benada
A modern approach to the traditional Czech gastronomy, Benada offers different menus for breakfast, weekends and business events. ❧ *Dlouhá 30* • *Map N2* • *296 398163* • **KKKK**

2 Paneria
Pick up ready-made sandwiches for a picnic on the steps of the nearby Rudolfinum *(see p36)*. You'll find branches of Paneria throughout the city. ❧ *Kaprova 3* • *Map K3* • *No credit cards* • **K**

3 Les Moules
This Belgian beer café offers typical brasserie fare along with a variety of seafood dishes. There is also a good selection of French cheeses. ❧ *Pařížská 19* • *Map L2* • *222 315022* • *Dis. access* • **KKKKK**

4 Ambroisie Caffè
Located in the Burzovní Palace, Ambroisie combines modern design with a lush garden in the atrium. On the menu are soups and salads, as well as meat, fish and pasta dishes. ❧ *Rybná 14* • *Map N3* • *221 842121* • *Open Mon–Fri* • **KKK**

5 La Bodeguita del Medio
This Cuban-Creole restaurant offers grilled fish and meats using authentic ingredients. Popular with the business crowd, it boasts a great atmosphere and welcoming staff. ❧ *Kaprova 5* • *Map K3* • *224 813922* • *Dis. access* • **KKKK**

6 King Solomon
Prague's foremost kosher restaurant has separate facilities for meat and dairy dishes. Closes for Friday sabbath. ❧ *Široká 8* • *Map L3* • *224 818752* • **KKKKK**

7 Pivnice u Pivrnce
A pub with wall decorations by Czech caricaturist Peter Urban. Choose from Czech specialities, or simply enjoy a beer. ❧ *Maiselova 3* • *Map L3* • *222 329404* • *Dis. access* • **KK**

8 Barock
With its floor-to-ceiling windows, Barock is the place to see and be seen. Join Prague's elite for a good cocktail. ❧ *Pařížská 24* • *Map L2* • *222 329221* • **KKKKK**

9 Modrá Zahrada
Usually crowded with people enjoying the large, thin-crust pizzas. ❧ *Široká 18* • *Map L2* • **KK**

10 Farrango
This Thai fusion restaurant not only offers great Thai cuisine but also dishes from Cambodia and Vietnam. ❧ *Dušní 15* • *Map L1* • *224 815996* • **KKKK**

Left **Roof detail, New Town Hall** Right **National Theatre**

New Town

FOUNDED IN 1348, *New Town* (Nové Město) *is hardly new. Charles IV's urban development scheme imposed straight avenues on the settlements springing up outside the old city walls and added a fourth town to the constellation of Old Town, Malá Strana and Hradčany. Unlike the Old Town, New Town was a planned grid of streets and markets. The horse market became Wenceslas Square in the 19th century; the 14th-century cattle market, and Europe's largest square, took on Charles's name, becoming Karlovo náměstí. The hay market, Senovážné náměstí, kept its title until the Communists changed it for a time to honour the Russian novelist Maxim Gorky. Since the Velvet Revolution was played out on Národní and Wenceslas Square, these and the surrounding streets have been filled with exciting enterprises.*

Statue, Franciscan Garden

🔟 Sights

1. Wenceslas Square
2. Náměstí Republiky
3. Na Příkopě
4. Franciscan Garden
5. Národní třída
6. National Theatre
7. The Dancing House
8. Karlovo náměstí
9. New Town Hall
10. Palackého náměstí

Although some locals still call Senovážné náměstí "Gorkáč", it has returned to its old name on maps.

1 Wenceslas Square

This former horse market, in contrast to its medieval counterpart in the Old Town (see pp14–17), expresses the history of 20th-century Prague, from its beautiful Art Nouveau façades to the memories of the many marches,

Na Příkopě

political protests and celebrations that have shaped the city over the past 100 years (see pp30–31).

2 Náměstí Republiky

The odd couple of the Art Nouveau Municipal House and the Neo-Gothic Powder Tower are the centrepiece of Náměstí Republiky (Republic Square), facing the Czech National Bank's stern façade and the renovated Hybernia Theatre. Behind the theatre is the former home of the Lenin Museum, which was closed in 1991 after the Communists had lost power. In the northeast corner of the square stands Palladium, a unique shopping mall with the exterior of the former Franciscan Monastery and newly built interior. On the opposite side stands Kotva, a former socialist department store. ◎ Map P3

Náměstí Republiky

3 Na Příkopě

Formerly a moat protecting the city's eastern flank, Na Příkopě is Prague's fashion boulevard, counting Benetton, Gant, Korres (the only branch in the Czech Republic) and Guess among its big-name stores. Shoppers jam the pedestrian zone and pavement cafés, streaming between the gleaming Myslbek Shopping Centre and Slovanský dům, with its 10-screen multiplex cinema. The Hussite firebrand Jan Želivský preached on the site now occupied by another shopping mall, the Černá Růže Palace. ◎ Map N5

4 Franciscan Garden

The Franciscans moved into this area near Wenceslas Square in 1604, reclaiming the former Carmelite monastery. The grounds and nearby Church of Our Lady of the Snow had fallen into decay following the Hussite civil war, but the monks beautifully restored them. The gardens remained closed to the public until 1950, when the Communists thought they were worth sharing. Although there's little love lost for the dictatorship of the proletariat, the gardens remain popular with young couples and pigeon-feeding pensioners (see p41). ◎ Map N6

Karlovo náměstí

Národní třída
5 The end of Communism in Czechoslovakia began midway between the National Theatre and what is now the Tesco supermarket. On 17 November 1989, police put a brutal end to a pro-democracy march as it made its way to Wenceslas Square. A plaque under the arcade at Národní 20 marks where marchers and truncheons met. ◈ Map L6

National Theatre
6 Patriotic Czechs funded the theatre's construction twice: once in 1868 and again after fire destroyed the building in 1883. To see the stunning allegorical ceiling frescoes and Vojtěch Hynais' celebrated stage curtain,

Auditorium, National Theatre

take in one of the operas staged here; good picks are Smetana's *Libuše*, which debuted on this stage, or Dvořák's *The Devil and Kate*. Next door is Laterna Magika, where you can see black-light productions *(see p64)*. ◈ *Národní třída 2 • Map E4*

The Dancing House
7 Built in 1992–6, this edifice by Vlado Milunic and Frank Gehry is known as the Dancing House, or "Ginger and Fred", due to its iconic towers, which resemble two dancers. The majority of the building is given over to offices and closed to the public, but the 7th floor restaurant, Céleste, open to everyone, offers magnificent views of Prague Castle and the Vltava River. ◈ *Rašínovo nábřeží 80 • Map E6*

Karlovo náměstí
8 Charles IV had his city planners build New Town's central square to the same dimensions as Jerusalem's. Originally a cattle market, it's now a park popular with dog-walkers. Among the trees are monuments to such luminaries as Eliška Krásnohorská, who wrote libretti for Smetana's operas. To the west, on Resslova, is the Church of Sts Cyril and Methodius. The members of the Czech resistance, responsible for the assassination of Nazi leader Reinhard Heydrich (1904–42), took refuge here *(see p39)*. ◈ Map F5

9 New Town Hall

In 1419, an anti-clerical mob led by Jan Želivský hurled the Catholic mayor and his councillors from a New Town Hall window in the first of Prague's defenestrations *(see p11)*. The Gothic tower on the building's eastern end was added a few years later; its viewing platform is open to the public. Crowds gather round the tower's base most Saturdays to congratulate newlyweds, married in the building's Gothic hall. ⊗ *Karlovo náměstí 23 • Map F5 • Tower open Apr–Oct 10am–6pm Tue–Sun • Adm*

10 Palackého náměstí

The riverside square is named for the 19th-century historian František Palacký, whose work was integral to the National Revival. Stanislav Suchard's sweeping monument to him stands at the plaza's northern end, while the modern steeples of the Emaus Monastery rise from the eastern edge *(see p52)*. The church grounds are also known as the Slavonic Monastery, named after the liturgy the resident Balkan Benedictines used. Sadly, American bombs demolished the monastery's original Baroque steeples on St Valentine's Day 1945, as part of the Allies' World War II military campaign. ⊗ *Map E6*

Emaus Monastery, Palackého náměstí

A Day in New Town

Morning

After breakfast at **Hotel Evropa** *(see p78)*, head to **Wenceslas Square** *(see pp30–31)* to begin the day's sightseeing. A quick peep inside the **National Museum** *(see p36)* will probably suffice unless it's raining or you're a big fan of natural history. From there, proceed to St Wenceslas's statue and the monument to Communism's victims, where you can pay tribute to the nation's growing pains.

Get in a bit of retail therapy along the square as you walk up to Můstek, then visit the **Museum of Communism** *(see p110)*, ironically located above McDonald's and a casino.

Walk down to the river. Enjoy the view of the Post-Modern Dancing House, then have lunch at **Restaurace U Pomníku** *(see p113)*.

Afternoon

After lunch, head up to the **National Theatre** and then follow the Vltava's Right Bank upstream to Jiráskovo náměstí. Modern-art buffs should take in **Galerie Mánes** *(see p110)* on the way. Follow Resslova up the hill to the **Church of Sts Cyril and Methodius** and its monument to Czechoslovak resistance fighters.

In the evening, take in a performance at the National Theatre; **U Matěje Kotrby** *(see p112)* is the obvious choice for dinner, before or after. If you still have the energy, head to **Radost FX** *(see p111)* to dance the night away or to **U Havrana** *(see p112)* for a local, smoky atmosphere.

Following pages: **National Museum and Wenceslas statue at night**

Left **Galerie Mánes** Right **Dvořák Museum**

TOP 10 Galleries and Museums

1 Galerie Mánes
Occupying the southern tip of Žofín Island, this contemporary art gallery hosts both Czech and foreign artists. ◈ *Masarykovo nábřeží 250 • Map E5 • Open 10am–6pm Tue–Sun • Adm*

2 Galerie Via Art
Founded in 1991 as one of the first private galleries in Prague, this venue exhibits contemporary Czech paintings, sculptures and mixed-media art. It also arranges international exhibitions and artist exchanges. ◈ *Resslova 6 • Map E6 • Open 1–6pm Mon–Fri*

3 Postage Stamp Museum
Philatelists' mouths water over this one. Its exhibitions illustrate the colourful history of postage stamps in the Czech Republic and Europe. Sells commemorative sheets and graphic works too. ◈ *Nové mlýny 2 • Map G4 • Open 9am–noon, 1–5pm Tue–Sun • Adm*

4 Museum of the City of Prague
Visitors can explore 19th-century Prague with Antonín Langweil's scaled replica of the city. ◈ *Na Poříčí 52 • Map P3 • Open 9am–6pm Tue–Sun • Adm*

5 Mucha Museum
Art Nouveau artist Alfons Mucha is a national hero. Here you'll find his journals, sketchbooks and paintings, both private and commercial. ◈ *Panská 7 • Map N5 • Open 10am–6pm daily • Adm*

6 Museum of Communism
A triptych of the dream, reality and nightmare that was Communist Czechoslovakia. To fill the museum, its creators combed the country for mementos of its totalitarian past. ◈ *Na Příkopě 10 • Map F3 • Open 9am–9pm daily • Adm*

7 Václav Špála Gallery
This contemporary gallery exhibits works mainly by local artists. Its aim is to make art more accessible to the general public by striving to establish a relationship between the two. ◈ *Národní třída 30 • Map L6*

8 National Museum
Palaeontology, mineralogy and a host of other "ologies". The museum's collections are scattered throughout the country, but the Wenceslas Square edifice is a cultural artifact in its own right *(see p36)*. ◈ *Václavské náměstí 68 • Map G5 • Open 10am–6pm daily • Adm*

9 Police Museum
The museum documents the police's efforts with engaging exhibits, such as an interactive crime scene. ◈ *Ke Karlovu 1 • Map G6 • Open 10am–5pm Tue–Sun • Adm*

10 Dvořák Museum
This Baroque palace houses the 19th-century composer's piano and viola, as well as other memorabilia of his life and work *(see p45)*. ◈ *Ke Karlovu 20 • Map G6 • Open 10am–5pm Tue–Sun • Adm*

Left **Radost FX** Right **Nebe (Heaven)**

🔟 Nightspots

1 Radost FX
Late at night, club kids take over the disco, lounge and café. By day, a broader demographic comes for the good vegetarian food. Sunday brunch is especially popular. Open until 4am *(see p66)*.
◈ *Bělehradská 120 • Map G6*

2 Beer Factory
Walk down the lit glass staircase to this venue, where you will be welcomed by a friendly and relaxed atmosphere. You can tap your own beer here.
◈ *Václavské náměstí 58 • Map G4*

3 Jazz Republic
Prague's leading music club features live jazz, funk, blues, dance, Latin, fusion or world music seven nights a week. The music programme varies every month. ◈ *28 října 1 • Map M6*

4 Lucerna
The granddaddy of Prague's clubs, the cavernous Lucerna hosts live jazz as well as rock and dance parties, including the ever popular 1980s and 1990s nights *(see p67)*.

5 Escape Club
If you want to step out for drinks and meet interesting people, then this gay club is the perfect place. Expect oil shows, striptease performances, dance shows, drinking games and much more. ◈ *V Jámě 8 • Map F5*

6 Nebe (Heaven)
This atmospheric club in an original stone cellar features stylish lighting and a gracefully curvaceous long bar. A separate lounge is a popular place for various private events.
◈ *Křemencova 10 • Map E5*

7 Reduta Jazz Club
Many celebrated musicians have played here, as has former US President Bill Clinton. Come here to hear all types of jazz from swing bands to modern styles. ◈ *Národní třída 20 • Map L6*

8 Duplex Dine & Dance
During the day, Duplex is an ideal location for lunch or dinner with nice views of the city. At night it turns into one of Prague's most exclusive clubs.
◈ *Václavské náměstí 21 • Map N6*

9 Ultramarin
The ground floor is a simple, convivial bar and restaurant. After you've had your fill, you'll find a music club downstairs, where you can dance. Open until 2am. ◈ *Ostrovní 32 • Map E4*

10 Billiard centrum v Cípu
Close to 100 billiard, pool and snooker tables, plus four lanes of bowling and two table-tennis sets. If going on Friday or Saturday, it is best to make a reservation – this place can get crowded. The bar serves drinks only.
◈ *V Cípu 1 • Map P5*

Left **The Globe Bookstore and Coffeehouse** Right **U Fleků**

🔟 Cafés and Pubs

1 The Globe Bookstore and Coffeehouse
The quality of the food varies with the Globe's mercurial staff, but the overall trend is upwards. Weekend brunch is the best time to visit. ⓢ *Pštrossova 6 • Map E5 • 224 934203*

2 Solidní Jistota
The name is bigger than the café. Serves good coffee, homemade pastries and a dozen flavours of ice cream. ⓢ *Pštrossova 21 • Map E5*

3 U Fleků
Exactly what you might expect from the city that created the "Beer-Barrel Polka". U Fleků is probably the city's most popular beer hall, and the prices reflect it *(see p60)*. ⓢ *Křemencova 11 • Map E5*

4 Novoměstský Pivovar
Enter this great place to expand your knowledge of beer. Classic Czech dishes are served in a working brewery. ⓢ *Vodičkova 20 • Map F4 • 222 232448*

5 Hostinec U Kalicha
This pub's decor and cartooned walls are based on the Czech novel *The Good Soldier Švejk*. Author Jaroslav Hašek *(see p44)* set some of the pivotal scenes here. ⓢ *Na bojišti 12–14 • KK*

6 U Matěje Kotrby
This lovely bar and restaurant with an old-world feel serves Czech-style meals, cold Pilsner and local wines. ⓢ *Křemencova 1738/17 • Map E5 • 224 930768 • KK*

7 Rocky O'Reilly's
Offering all a Celtophile could ask for, this lively pub has live music in the evenings, football on the TV, a roaring fire and plenty of stout. The food's fair as well. ⓢ *Štěpánská 32 • Map F5*

8 Café Louvre
Franz Kafka, Max Brod and their writer friends used to hold court here. It's a bright, cheerful place, good for conversation and a bite to eat. At the back is Prague's classiest pool hall. ⓢ *Národní 20 • Map L6 • KK*

9 Café 35
Students at the Institut Français and other Francophones gather here for coffee, quiche and a read of the French newspapers. The garden is a peaceful spot on sunny days. ⓢ *Štěpánská 35 • Map F5*

10 U Havrana
One of a dying breed, the Raven serves some of the best greasy food in town and a superior half-litre of beer. It is open until 5am. ⓢ *Hálkova 6 • Map G5*

Above **Restaurace U Pomníku**

🔟 Restaurants

Dynamo
This Post-Modern diner serves dishes such as rump steak in marinade with thyme and oregano. A wide selection of vegetarian options. 🕲 *Pštrossova 29* • *Map E5* • *224 932020* • **KK**

Restaurace Bredovský dvůr
Enjoy traditional Czech dishes such as game goulash with Karlsbad dumplings. In the summer, you can eat alfresco. 🕲 *Politických vězňů 13* • *Map P6* • **KKK**

Universal
A popular eatery, serving substantial meals at small prices. The café is especially recommended for its vegetarian dishes. 🕲 *V Jirchářích* • *Map E4* • *224 934416* • *Dis. access* • **KKK**

Restaurace U Pomníku
This Czech eatery serves traditional food and has a nostalgic atmosphere. Try the lunchtime specials (the menu changes every day) or the *à la carte* dinner. 🕲 *Gorazdova 1* • *224 923301* • **KK**

U Pinkasů
A great-value Czech beer hall since 1843, this is a very popular lunchtime destination. The food is simple but hearty, and the atmosphere lively. 🕲 *Jungmannovo náměstí 16* • *Map F4* • *221 111152* • **KKK**

Modrý Zub
Fast Thai food at its best, for a quick snack or light meal. Huge windows create a great opportunity for people watching. 🕲 *Jindřišská 5* • *Map P6* • *222 212622* • *Dis. access* • **KKK**

Lemon Leaf
Serving Thai and Burmese specials, the ingredients used are fresh and the presentation is colourful. Service is fast and friendly. 🕲 *Myslíkova 14* • *Map E5* • *224 919056* • *Dis. access* • **KK**

Jáma Restaurace
Jáma offers delicious Tex-Mex and American specialities and a fun atmosphere. Watch sporting events on several plasma screens dotted around the room. 🕲 *V jámě 7* • *Map F4* • *222 967081* • **KKK**

Trattoria Cicala
This authentic Italian eatery is a magnet for visiting film stars and other VIPs. The fresh pasta dishes can't be beaten. 🕲 *Žitná 43* • *Map F5* • *222 210375* • *Dis. access* • **KKKK**

Čestr
This is the perfect gourmet dinner choice before or after a night at the State Opera. The traditional beef steaks are delicious. 🕲 *Legerova 75* • *Map G6* • *222 727851* • **KKKKK**

Note: Unless otherwise stated, all restaurants accept credit cards and serve vegetarian meals

Left **Holešovice** Right **View of Prague from Smíchov**

Greater Prague

PRAGUE'S CITY CENTRE CAN KEEP MOST VISITORS occupied for days, but if you're staying outside the city's heart, or if you have the time to explore beyond the capital's walls, the outlying areas offer plenty of surprises. Over the centuries, Prague's various rulers have used the surrounding countryside as their personal playground, building impressive castles, palaces and parks to which they could escape the often claustrophobic streets and winding alleyways of the city. Even the Communists have left their own kind of functional mark on the area, with useful edifices, towers and exhibition spaces. From the peaceful parklands of Vyšehrad or the social atmosphere of Letná, to the rowdy nightlife of Žižkov and the intriguing gardens of Holešovice and Troja, Greater Prague has a diversity that will fulfil almost any requirements you might have.

Troja Château

🔟 Sights

1. Vyšehrad
2. Smíchov
3. Vinohrady
4. Holešovice
5. Letná Park
6. Stromovka
7. Troja
8. Výstaviště
9. National Memorial on the Vítkov Hill
10. Žižkov TV Tower

1 Vyšehrad

The former fortress of Vyšehrad *(see p121)* is steeped in legend. Bedřich Smetana paid tribute to the second seat of the Přemyslid dynasty that resided here in the 10th century in his opera *Libuše* and in his rousing patriotic work *Má vlast (see p44)*. The composer is buried here in the National Cemetery, as are many other luminaries of Czech culture. ◎ *Map B6*

Vinohrady

2 Smíchov

Today, modern shopping centres and multiplex cinemas have taken over what used to be the city's main industrial centre. At the heart of the district is Anděl metro station, which still bears traces of its Communist origins – the station was originally named "Moscow" and was decorated with Soviet murals *(see p49)*. ◎ *Map A6*

3 Vinohrady

Originally the royal vineyards, Vinohrady today is a gently rolling residential neighbourhood. The central square, Náměstí Míru, features the Neo-Gothic Church of St Ludmila and the Art Nouveau Vinohrady Theatre. For a bit of peace and greenery visit the Havlíčkovy sady. ◎ *Map B6*

4 Holešovice

Developers are helping this former warehouse district make a comeback. It's home to the National Gallery's Trade Fair Palace *(see pp26–7)*, and motor car fans will love the National Technical Museum, with its exhibits of Czech interwar vehicles such as Škodas. ◎ *Map B5 • National Technical Museum: Kostelní 42; Open 9am–5:30pm Tue–Fri, 10am–6pm Sat & Sun • Adm • Dis. access*

5 Letná Park

A grand staircase leads from the Vltava riverbank opposite the Josefov quarter *(see pp98–103)* to a giant metronome. The needle marks time where a mammoth statue of Joseph Stalin once stood before it was demolished in the 1960s *(see p48)*. The surrounding park echoes with the clatter of skateboards and barking dogs. Travelling circuses sometimes set up in the open fields, but Letná's popular beer garden is probably its biggest draw. ◎ *Map E1*

Čechův Most, with Letná Park in the background

Around Town – Greater Prague

Žižkov

This working-class neighbourhood came into being when city fathers divided the expanding Královské Vinohrady district. The inhabitants of the area thumbed their noses at Habsburg rule and named their new district after the Hussite warrior. Žižkovites' contrary nature runs deep, even having a separatist movement which promotes an independent Republic of Žižkov. An alternative culture thrives around the Akropolis club and the Divus artists collective, and increasingly, numerous ethnic restaurants are bringing an international flavour to the area.

Stromovka

King Otakar established the royal game park here in the 13th century; it's been a public garden since 1804 (*stromovka* means "place of trees"). Stroll, skate or simply enjoy the ancient trees by day and visit the planetarium by night. The fish ponds were a creation of Rudolf II – the emperor drilled a tunnel under Letná to bring in water to supply them (*see p41*). ⬥ *Map B5*

Troja

The riverside gardens and château of Troja are an excellent destination for a day trip. Cross the Vltava from Stromovka, take in the château's beautiful garden and art collection (*see p120*), the Baroque chapel of St Clare and the zoological gardens. There is a bus from here that will take you to the nearest metro station (Nádraží Holešovice). ⬥ *Map B5*

Výstaviště

The fairgrounds here were originally built at the end of the 19th century to host trade shows, but nowadays you're more likely to see a hockey match or a rock concert at Tesla Arena, or a Shakespeare performance at a replica of London's Globe Theatre. There's an amusement park with rides for the kids, an outdoor cinema and the oddly charming musical Křižík Fountain (*see p51*). If you want to see the original statues that graced Charles Bridge, rather than today's replicas, pay a visit to the Lapidárium, where they are preserved (*see p120*). ⬥ *Map B5*

National Memorial on the Vítkov Hill

View of the Žižkov Tower

9 National Memorial on the Vítkov Hill

The one-eyed Hussite general Jan Žižka defeated invading crusaders in 1420 atop the hill where his giant equestrian statue now stands in front of the Tomb of the Unknown Soldier. Erected in 1929, the monument serves as a memorial to all those who suffered in the Czech struggle for independence. The Communists co-opted the building, and for a time it served as President Klement Gottwald's mausoleum (see p48). ⓢ Žižkov • Map B6 • Open 10am–6pm Wed–Sun • Adm

10 Žižkov TV Tower

The Communists unashamedly cleared away a Jewish cemetery on the site in the 1970s to make way for this eyesore, reaching 216 m (709 ft) in height. However it didn't begin transmitting until after the Velvet Revolution. Despite a viewing platform, the tower is actually too tall to see anything clearly, but thrill-seekers may want to try. ⓢ Mahlerovy sady
• Map B6 • Open 8am–midnight
• Dis. access • Adm

Three Afternoons in Greater Prague

Afternoon One

🕐 See **Vyšehrad** (see p115) late in the day, but only if the weather looks promising. Take the metro to the Vyšehrad stop at the Congress Centre, from which you have marvellous views of Prague's spires. Walk west along Na Bučance and enter the fortifications through the **Tábor Gate** (see p121). Once inside the walls, you'll find historic constructions everywhere you turn, such as the Romanesque **Rotunda of St Martin** (see p121). Enjoy the park at your leisure but get to the westernmost edge of the compound atop Vyšehrad's rocky outcrop in time for a sunset.

Afternoon Two

Žižkov and **Vinohrady** (see p115) are also best seen in the second half of the day. From Florenc metro, climb to the **National Memorial on the Vítkov Hill** for a wonderful view, then compare it to the one you get from the **Žižkov TV Tower**. Stroll as far into Vinohrady as your feet will permit you, but save your strength: you'll need it for a night of pubbing and clubbing.

Afternoon Three

Energetic walkers can see **Stromovka** and **Troja** in a half-day. Take the tram to **Výstaviště** among the trees of the former game park before crossing the Vltava to the **Troja Château** (see p120). From there, you're within easy walking distance of the zoo. Take bus 112 back to the metro at Nádraží Holešovice.

Following pages: **Troja Château**

117

Left **Troja Chateau** Centre **Bertramka** Right **Olšany Cemetery**

🔟 Best of the Rest

1 Lapidarium
This is where Prague's statues go when they retire. Among the 700-plus items is the original St Wenceslas from Wenceslas Square. ✆ *Výstaviště 422, Holešovice • Map B5 • Open noon–6pm Wed–Sun • Dis. access • Adm*

2 Troja Château
Jean-Baptiste Mathey created Count Sternberg's 17th-century palace when Classical Italian was the rage. It has a collection of 19th-century Czech art. ✆ *U Trojského zámku 1, Troja • Map B5 • Open Apr–Oct: 10am–6pm Tue–Sun; Nov–Mar: 10am–5pm Sat–Sun • Adm*

3 Troja Zoo
Prague's zoological gardens date back to 1931. The most popular exhibits are the big cats and gorillas. ✆ *U Trojského zámku 120, Troja • Map B5 • Zoo: Jun–Aug: 9am–7pm; Apr, May, Sep, Oct: 9am–6pm; Nov–Feb: 9am–4pm; Mar: 9am–5pm • Adm*

4 Břevnov Monastery
St Adalbert founded this Benedictine monastery in 993. You can see remains of the Romanesque church, and the 18th-century church of St Margaret. ✆ *Markétská 28, Břevnov • Map B5 • 220 406111 • Guided visits (in Czech): Apr–Oct: 10am, 2 & 4pm Sat & Sun; Nov–Mar: 10am & 2pm Sat & Sun • Adm*

5 Bertramka
The house where Mozart and his wife stayed while the composer worked on *Don Giovanni* has been turned into a small museum about his life. ✆ *Mozartova 169, Smíchov • Map A6 • Open 10am–3pm Tue–Sun • Adm*

6 Barrandov Studios
Once a Nazi and Communist propaganda mill, today the studios are thriving as western filmmakers discover Prague *(see pp46–7)*. ✆ *Kříženeckého náměstí 5, Barrandov • 267 071111 • Open by appt*

7 Olšany Cemetery
Plague victims were interred here when the site was still far from the city. Other notable residents include Jan Palach, a student who burned himself alive in protest at the 1968 Warsaw-Pact invasion. ✆ *Vinohradská 153 • Map B6 • Open 8am–5pm; Mar, Apr, Oct: 8am–6pm; May–Sep: 8am–7pm*

8 New Jewish Cemetery
Franz Kafka's memorial is here, as are those of Prague Jews who died in the Holocaust *(see p25)*. ✆ *Izraelská 1 • Map B6 • Open 9am–4pm Sun–Thu; Apr–Sep: 9am–5pm*

9 Slapy Reservoir
The dam in the Vltava not only helps prevent flooding, it makes a nice swimming and boating reserve. ✆ *Map B5*

10 Panelaks
The majority of Prague's residents still live in these prefab estates after moving here during the urbanization process of the and1980s. ✆ *Map B5*

Don't miss the chairlift ride over the whole complex of Troja Zoo – great for kids.

Left **Church of Sts Peter and Paul** Right **Rotunda of St Martin**

TOP 10 Vyšehrad Sights

1 Church of Sts Peter and Paul
Although the first church to stand on this site was founded by Vratislav II in the 11th century, the Neo-Gothic structure seen today dates from 1903. The very valuable Gothic altar with a panel depicting *Our Lady of the Rains* is on the right-hand side of the chapel. ⊗ *Štulcova • Metro Vyšehrad • Open 10am–6pm Mon–Sat, 10:30am–6pm Sun*

2 Slavín Monument
This is the burial place of several notable Czech cultural figures, and students laid flowers in remembrance here on 17 November 1989, before marching into town for the Velvet Revolution *(see p35)*. ⊗ *K Rotundě • Metro Vyšehrad • Open Jan, Feb, Nov, Dec: 8am–5pm; Mar, Apr, Oct: 8am–6pm; May–Sep: 8am–7pm*

3 Devil's Pillar
The story goes that the devil bet a local priest that he could carry this pillar from the Church of St Mary to Rome before the clergyman could finish his sermon. Being a sore loser, Satan threw the column to the ground here. ⊗ *K Rotundě • Metro Vyšehrad*

4 Casements
In the 18th century, occupying French troops drilled holes in Vyšehrad rock to store ammunition. ⊗ *Metro Vyšehrad*

5 Rotunda of St Martin
This 11th-century chapel is the oldest in Prague and most likely to be the oldest Christian house of worship in the country. It was reconstructed in 1878. ⊗ *K Rotundě • Metro Vyšehrad*

6 Tábor Gate (Špička)
Charles IV restored Vyšehrad's fortifications in the 14th century. Catholic crusaders rode through this gate on their way to crush the Táborites in 1434. ⊗ *V Pevnosti • Metro Vyšehrad*

7 Congress Centre
This ex-Communist palace of culture now hosts international conferences as well as pop concerts *(see p49)*. ⊗ *Metro Vyšehrad*

8 Nusle Bridge
This simple, utilitarian viaduct spans the Nusle Valley, connecting New Town to the Pankrác banking and commercial district. ⊗ *Metro Vyšehrad*

9 Cubist Houses
Josef Chochol built the angular buildings on Rašínovo nábřeží, Libušina and the corner of Přemyslova and Neklanova. ⊗ *Metro Vyšehrad*

10 Smetana's Grave
At the start of each year's Prague Spring International Music Festival *(see p68)*, musicians attend a ceremony at composer Bedřich Smetana's grave. ⊗ *Metro Vyšehrad*

Left **Hlučná samota** Right **U Vystřeleného Oka**

TOP 10 Cafés and Pubs

1 La Creperie
This French-owned café does a solid business of crêpes, waffles and other Gallic delicacies. A nice selection of French and other imported wines, too.
Ⓢ *Janovského 4, Holešovice • Map B5*

2 U Vystřeleného Oka
The name "At the Shot-Out Eye" is a tribute to the half-blind Hussite general Jan Žižka from whom Žižkov takes its name and whose enormous statue looms overhead *(see p117)*. Ⓢ *U Božích bojovníků 3, Žižkov • Map B6*

3 U Holanů
Tuck into a plate of pickled sausages or herring at Vinohrady's favourite no-nonsense pub. Simple but clean, with perfunctory service; they don't make them like this anymore.
Ⓢ *Londýnská 10, Vinohrady • Map B6*

4 U Houdků
This hidden little gem in Žižkov serves Czech meals that are great value for money. In summer you can sit outside.
Ⓢ *Bořivojova 110, Žižkov • Map B5 • 222 711239 • No credit cards • K*

5 Hospůdka nad Viktorkou
Bořivojova street boasts more pubs per metre than any other place in the country, and possibly the world. There's nothing elegant about nad Viktorkou, but it's the ultimate Prague pub. Ⓢ *Bořivojova 79, Žižkov • Map B6*

6 Potrefená husa
"The Wounded Goose", as Potrefená husa translates, is the place to go to watch football over local delicacies. Several domestic and imported beers are available for a loud and lively clientele. Ⓢ *Resslova 1 • Map E5*

7 Pastička
"The Mousetrap" is a perfect blend of old-fashioned beer hall and modish gastro-pub. Visit it for a choice of light and dark Bernard beer and good, filling food. Ⓢ *Blanická 25, Vinohrady • Map B6*

8 Café Faux Pas
Start the day at this café which opens at 8am, serving a variety of sweet and savoury crêpes and fresh sandwiches.
Ⓢ *Vinohradská 31 • Map H5*

9 Hlučná samota
This refined pub takes its name from Bohumil Hrabal's novel *Too Loud a Solitude (see p45)*. Neither loud nor solitary, guests return time and again for the excellent beer and food.
Ⓢ *Zahřebská 14, Vinohrady • Map B6*

10 Carpe Diem
This establishment comprises a coffee shop, a jazz/folk music bar and an art gallery all under one roof. The Italian Vergnano coffee is particularly recommended.
Ⓢ *Jičínská 4 • Map B5 • 272 741421*

Around Town – Greater Prague

Price Categories

For a three-course meal for one with half a bottle of wine (or equivalent meal), taxes and extra charges.

K	under Kč300
KK	Kč300–Kč500
KKK	Kč500–Kč700
KKKK	Kč700–Kč1000
KKKKK	over Kč1000

Above **Aromi**

🔟 Restaurants

1 Aromi
This Italian restaurant serves authentic food accompanied by a great range of wines from around the world. ✆ *Manesova 78, Prague 2* • *Map H5* • *222 713222* • *Dis. access* • **KKKKK**

2 Olympos
Prague's best Greek food. The large garden, complete with table tennis, is ideal for summer dining. The mixed salad platter is the best value around.
✆ *Kubelíkova 9, Žižkov* • *Map B6* • *222 722239* • *Dis. access* • **KKK**

3 Mailsi
This little Pakistani eatery offers better value than the Indian restaurants in the centre. Close to the No. 9 tram stop, it's not as remote as it appears.
✆ *Lipanská 1, Žižkov* • *Map B6* • *222 717783* • *No credit cards* • **KKK**

4 Rana
When Mehfooz Ahmed sold Mailsi to his brother, his fans followed him here, where he serves up the best curries in town. The vindaloo is for true spice devotees. ✆ *Na Dědince 12, Palmovka* • *721 809084* • *No credit cards* • *Dis. access* • **K**

5 Koliba Praha
Enjoy traditional Czech and Slovak specialities and a good choice of wines. At the weekend, evenings are enlivened by a Romany band. ✆ *Gregorova 8, Horní Roztyly* • *Map B5* • *272 941340* • **KKK**

6 Hotel Diana
It's a trek getting here, but Hotel Diana wins the prize for the best game restaurant. The dill-and-potato *kulajda* soup is a must. Try the boar, too. ✆ *Hůrská 12, Prague 9* • *281 867206* • **KKKK**

7 Restaurant Daliborka
Club Hotel Daliborka's elegant in-house restaurant is something of a local culinary secret. Have stewed veal cheeks under the ancient chestnut trees and you'll see why many would like it to stay that way.
✆ *K Novému dvoru 124, Prague 4* • *261 711307* • **KKKKK**

8 U Cedru
For an authentic Lebanese dining experience order a spread of hummus, tabbouleh and other appetizers with pitta. ✆ *Národní Obrany 27, Dejvice* • *233 342974* • **KKK**

9 Máneska
Steaks, salads, ribs and other American dishes keep tables full here. Reservations are a must. The menu changes regularly, but the chocolate fondue will always remain. ✆ *Mánesova 59, Vinohrady* • *Map B6* • *222 212052* • **KKKKK**

10 U Marčanů
Folk music and dancing make this restaurant a fun lunch spot. Large portions of Czech food are served at communal tables. It is a fair way from the city, so book ahead and take a taxi. ✆ *Veleslavínská 14, Prague 6* • *Map B5* • *235 360623* • **KK**

Note: Unless otherwise stated, all restaurants accept credit cards and serve vegetarian meals

STREETSMART

PRAGUE'S TOP 10

Left **Ruzyně Airport** Right **Hlavní Nádraží central station**

🔟 Getting to Prague

By Air
More than 40 international airlines fly to Prague's Ruzyně airport. The national carrier Czech Airlines (ČSA) is a member of the Sky Team alliance, whose members include Delta, Air France and Alitalia. Direct flights from London are about 2 hours; from New York, about 9 hours. 🌎 *ČSA: 239 007007 • www.csa.cz*

Ruzyně Airport
Located 15 km (9 miles) northwest of the city centre, Ruzyně is Prague's only international airport. Until 1989, a red neon hammer-and-sickle greeted visitors landing here. There are all the modern facilities here now, though, including car rental offices, bureaux de change, shops and restaurants. Municipal buses serve the airport, and there is also an airport express bus (costing Kč60) and the Cedaz minibus service (Kč150).

By Train
Prague is on major European rail routes; the Orient Express's London–Paris–Venice route passes through town. International trains to the Czech capital are comfortable, with couchette sleeping facilities, fast excepting delays during snow, and are an alternative to flying if you have time.

By Coach
Coaches are your best bet for long journeys on a budget. These buses are reasonably priced and very comfortable. 🌎 *www.studentagency.cz • www.eurolines.cz • www.orangeways.com*

By Car
If you're going to be driving in the Czech Republic for more than 30 days, you'll need an international driver's licence. If you bring your own car, you must carry a vehicle registration card and a red warning triangle, and display a national identification sticker. Several motorways and speedways spread from Prague radially to different corners of the country.

Customs
Visitors from outside the EU can bring goods worth less than €175 (about Kč5,000) into the country without paying a duty. Two litres or less of wine, one litre of spirits and 200 cigarettes (or their equivalent in tobacco) can also be brought in duty free.

Discount Deals
Travellers from the UK should check with easyJet, Ryanair or Wizz Air for return tickets to Prague at reasonable prices. Czech Airlines offers discounts on some of its flights.

🌎 *Czech Airlines: www.csa.cz • easyJet: www.easyjet.com • Ryanair: www.ryanair.com • Wizz Air: www.wizzair.com*

Visas and Passports
Most visitors may stay visa-free in the Czech Republic for up to 90 days, but it is always wise to confirm this with the Czech embassy in your own country or check with your travel agent for up-to-date visa requirements. Czech immigration officials may request you to be carrying at least Kč1,100 per day for your visit (or have a valid credit card).

When to Go
Prague teems with tourists during the summer. However, the best time to travel is during the spring and autumn months, which is when the city is at its most picturesque – though hotels are at their most expensive.

Long Stays
If you choose to stay longer than 90 days, you'll need to apply for a long-term visa, valid for a year. For this, you'll need proof of employment, health insurance and housing as well as a clean criminal record. This visa can be renewed annually for eight years, after which you can apply for permanent residency.

Left **Prague metro station** Right **Prague tram**

Getting Around Prague

1 Metro

Prague's underground transit system is fast, efficient and, with a little practice, easy to navigate. There are three lines, known as A, B and C; or more commonly, green, yellow and red. Validate your ticket, available from vending machines at the stations' vestibules, at the ticket barriers. These passes are valid for all Prague public transport.

2 Tram

Prague trams make it easy to see much of the city while saving you shoe leather. The schedules can be a little tricky to read, however, and re-routings are frequent. Buy tickets in advance – they are available all over the city from newsagents, and from metro stations.

3 Buses

Buses serve outlying areas – they are banned from the centre because of pollution. As with trams, riders must validate their tickets by using the punching machines on the bus. For some stops, riders must notify the driver of their intention to get off by pressing a button near the door.

4 Taxis

Prague's taxis have received a lot of bad press *(see p129)*, but most firms are now reliable. Phone a central despatcher in advance – your hotel will be able to give you a number – to be assured of safety and a fair price. If the car doesn't have a lighted sign with the word "Taxi" written on it, don't get in. And make sure the meter's running. Generally, avoid taxis that line up outside the major tourist sights.

5 Driving

Prague's city centre was not designed for the volume of traffic it sees nowadays. The streets are narrow and winding and parking is very scarce. If you must drive, keep to the right, wear a seatbelt, and be aware that traffic violations are payable on the spot. Illegally parked cars are regularly clamped or towed away by vigilant traffic wardens.

6 On Foot

Walking is the only way to see much of the city. The centre is only about 4 km (2.5 miles) from end to end and many of the historic sights, such as Prague Castle *(see pp8–11)* and the Old Town Square *(see pp14–17)* are in pedestrianized zones. Make sure you wear comfortable, flat-soled shoes, watch your step on the cobblestones, and look out for trams that drive in the centre of the road in both directions.

7 River Boats

A river cruise along the Vltava can offer a relaxing and romantic afternoon of sightseeing that's easy on weary feet. Tour boats depart from Čechův and Palackého bridges. You can also rent rowing boats near Charles Bridge.

8 Horse and Carriage

Horse and carriages line Old Town Square and take tourists for short rides through the surrounding streets. This can make a pleasant (and romantic) after-dinner diversion. Surprisingly, the horses don't seem to mind the crowds and auto traffic.

9 Cycling

While Prague has numerous bicycle routes, cyclists do not have their own lanes on the streets and must share the road with cars, which can prove hazardous. The cobblestones can also be hard going. Some services offer guided cycling tours of the city – check with the Prague Information Service *(see p128)*.

10 Guided Tours

While some guided tours are little more than a mob following a distant umbrella, many services offer personal insight to the city. Check with the Prague Information Service, or look for posters advertising pub crawls.

Left **The Prague Post** Right **Prague Information Service office**

🔟 Sources of Information

1 Prague Information Service

The Prague Information Service (PIS) serves as a central clearing house for information about all kinds of concerts, theatre performances and other cultural events. They literally have it all, from discos to art galleries, and publish it in a monthly guide available at their offices around town and on the Internet. They will also supply you with useful maps, and all the staff are English-speaking.
🔹 *Prague Information Service: Staroměstské náměstí 1, Main station Hlavní nádraží & Rytířská 31 • 221 714444 • www. praguewelcome.cz*

2 Čedok

The state-run tourist office has locations all over the city and can offer the usual advice required by tourists, such as hotel accommodation, cultural events and details of guided tours, both in Prague and outside the city. They have a lot of English-language material to hand out for free.
🔹 *Čedok: Na příkopě 18 • 800 112112 • www. cedok.cz*

3 The Prague Post

Don't listen to the jaded expatriates, who take pleasure in bringing this long-standing newspaper down. This English-language weekly has been publishing a fair semblance of news for over 20 years. The cinema, entertainment, exhibition and restaurant guides are well-nigh essential. There are also interesting articles on local politics and events. It is available from most newsstands. 🔹 *www. praguepost.cz*

4 Internet

A quick search for "Prague" on any search engine will give you links to hundreds of websites catering to Bohemians. These offer a variety of information about where to stay, weather reports, hotel accommodation, travel and much more.

5 Radio Prague

The foreign-language service of state-run Czech Radio, Radio Prague broadcasts news and features in English and six other languages. You can listen at www.radio.cz.

6 Přehled Kulturních Pořadů

The preferred publication of the Czech reader has got it all. Two hundred or so pages published every month list all events, concerts and clubs, as well as current exhibitions in museums and galleries. It is also useful if you want to find out what's playing at the nearest cinema.

7 Houser.cz

One of many counter-culture magazines on sale in the city, this free publication has been covering the city's club scene for more than five years. Although it's not necessarily credible, it's still entertaining. Definitely one for the twenty-something visitors to Prague who want to know about current nightlife.

8 Prague Tribune

An English-language trade and lifestyle monthly for the business professional is also of interest to tourists for its smart interviews with movers and shakers and fun reviews.

9 In Your Pocket

This bi-monthly mini-magazine is the perfect resource to find the best hotel or restaurant and also to discover what the city has to offer. It also contains travel advice and tips. *In Your Pocket* is available at newsstands across the city or online at www.inyour pocket.com.

10 Prague TV's City Guide

The website www. prague.tv offers lots of information about the city, covering everything from accommodation options to job vacancies and cinema listings.

Left **Crowds on Charles Bridge** Right **Taxis lined up at Wenceslas Square**

🔟 Things to Avoid

1 Midday on Charles Bridge
Unless you enjoy being packed cheek-to-jowl with fellow travellers, visit this popular spot *(see pp18–19)* sometime other than midday. The mobs start arriving around 10am, especially during summer. Early risers can have the bridge more or less to themselves at sunrise.

2 Pickpockets
Tourists are an easy target for petty thievery. Avoid any place where you'll be pressed up against strangers. Pickpockets on trams and metro cars have numerous routines to relieve travellers of their valuables. Have a copy of your passport and avoid carrying too much cash.

3 Unscrupulous Taxi Drivers
The best way to avoid being taken for a ride, as it were, is to phone a central despatcher *(see p127)* to send a car to you. Avoid using cars marked "transport", and those without pricing information posted on the door and never agree to "negotiate" a price – taxis should always have a meter running.

4 Two-Tiered Pricing
While it violates the law to charge tourists more, many reputable establishments, including the Jewish Museum *(see p99)*, offer a 50 per cent discount to Czechs. Simply letting ticket sellers know you're aware of the lower price helps, but it is still no real guarantee that you won't be penalized for being a foreigner.

5 Re-routed Trams
In a city as old as Prague, the infrastructure needs constant repair. This means tearing up streets and, inevitably, re-routing your tram. Before setting off, check for updates from the Prague public transport network at www.dpp.cz. To avoid confusion, timetables for re-routed trams are yellow instead of white.

6 Dog Mess
The municipal authorities gave up many years ago trying to count how many canine residents Prague has. It has also largely absolved itself of trying to clean up after them. Local dog-owners are also notoriously careless, so watch your step.

7 Prostitution
Despite the best intentions of the law, the oldest profession still thrives in a "grey zone" of the city. Never assume that prostitution is legal. Even saints should avoid prostitutes of both sexes: they are often known to supplement their incomes by picking pockets.

8 Non-Stop and Herna bars
Unfortunately, Prague has too few reputable bars and cafés open into the early hours. The words "non-stop" and *"herna"* are synonymous with shady characters; the latter are filled with slot machines and gambling addicts. You'd be better off getting an early night, or paying to get in to a nightclub.

9 Skinheads
Owing to 40 years of Communist isolation, some Czechs are sadly unaccustomed to people who do not look like them, or dress like them. Since 1989, the Neo-Nazi skinhead movement has grown at a disturbing rate. Random, unprovoked violence against dark-skinned individuals may occur, but it is unlikely to affect you in the main tourist areas.

10 Food Poisoning
Cases of lethal food poisoning are very rare, but mild cases are common; be familiar with the symptoms, such as nausea and diarrhoea. Stands selling food on the street are more likely to cause problems than proper restaurants, as the ingredients are exposed to bacteria and often not very well cooked. When in doubt, avoid fish, eggs and products including mayonnaise.

Left **Prague pension** Right **The Globe Bookstore**

🔟 Accommodation Tips

Off-season Prices
The peak tourist season runs roughly Apr–May and Sep–Oct, with another pocket of high prices around New Year and Easter; check whether prices have been hiked up for a particular event before booking. Prices are lower Jun–Aug. An accommodation company offers last-minute prices for numerous hotels; you can check their availability at www.accomgroup.com.

Bargain Districts
Exploring accommodation options outside the city centre can save you a considerable amount on your hotel bills. The neighbourhoods of Žižkov, Karlín, Smíchov and Holešovice, for example, all have good connections to the centre *(see pp114–17)* and an increasing number of good quality hotels.

Annonce
If you're staying a bit longer than the average tourist and want to save money on long-term accommodation, check the daily classified advertisement publication *Annonce*. Almost all the ads are in Czech, but if you can find someone to translate, you'll find affordable rooms and apartments for rent, both on short- and long-term agreements. *Annonce* is available from most newsagents.

Hotel Standards
If you recognize the name of your hotel (such as a chain hotel), you'll recognize the quality of the services and amenities; otherwise, be prepared for surprises. Not all hotel rooms have en suite bathrooms, for example, or plush bath towels. If such items are important to you, enquire before you book.

Things to Avoid
If you've failed to book a room in advance, go directly to a local travel agent or hotel. Do not accept accommodation from touts at the airport, train station or bus depot. Even if they're not out to rob you, you have no guarantee as to the quality of the rooms.

Parking
Smaller hotels may not have reserved parking spaces for guests. If this is the case, ask the management about the safest places to park. Never leave valuables in your car and make sure you're parked in a legal space; being towed or clamped can ruin precious holiday time.

Pets
Prague is a very pet-friendly city – good news for animal-owners and bad news for allergy sufferers. When you book, check whether you can bring pets; if you fear the fur, ask for assurances that your room hasn't been doubling up as a kennel recently.

Security
Whatever the destination, it almost goes without saying that tourists should use common sense when it comes to travelling with valuables – if possible, leave anything you wouldn't want to lose at home. In the better hotels, keep items such as passports and jewellery in the hotel safe. Be aware that even the best hotels can be targets of streetside scams.

Short-term Apartment Rentals
If you're staying a week or longer, you may want to skip the hotels entirely and rent a small flat. The Prague Information Service, state travel agency Čedok and numerous other local agencies can help you find a short-term rental *(see p128)*.

Finding a Flat
Many real estate companies offer sublets, long-term and month-to-month rentals. For a fee, usually the value of one month's rent, they can find you a home and help you with the necessary paperwork. If you want to go it on your own, check bulletin boards at The Globe Bookstore *(see p112)*.

Left **Vegetarian snack** Right **Prague café**

🔟 Eating and Drinking Tips

Vegetarian Tips
Meat- and dairy-free dining is no longer the problem it was a few years ago. Many new restaurants offer vegetarians a wide variety of tasty meatless meals, while older establishments are increasingly sensitive to vegetarians' needs. That said, never assume your vegetables won't come smothered with cheese. ◙ Lehká Hlava: Boršov 2 • Map K5 • 222 220665 • **KK**

Ordering
Except for the grander eateries, many Prague restaurants have yet to grasp multiple-course service. Emphasize that you want your appetizer (jako předkrm) before your main course. You will probably also have to order your side dish à la carte. Your steak will be well-done unless you plead otherwise.

Paying
Verify the restaurant takes credit cards before you order. Restaurants seldom accept travellers' cheques. Tell your waiter you'd like to pay with one word: zaplatím. You and your party may pay dohromady (all together) or zvlašť (separately).

Tipping
While tipping in Prague is approaching the international standard of 15 per cent, it is still common in pubs to simply round up the bill. If your beer and schnitzel cost Kč82, for example, pay Kč90. Rather than leaving the tip on the table, tell your waiter how much you want to give.

Making Reservations
Reserving a table is always a good idea and can save you a great deal of hungry wandering come dinner time. In many restaurants, it's common for lone diners to join other tables. If you're alone and want to know if a seat is free, point at it and ask "Je tu volno?"

Smoking
Prague restaurants are seldom non-smoking. A local ordinance bans smoking at lunch time, but it is seldom, if ever, enforced. For a smoke-free meal, try the vegetarian restaurants Country Life and Little Buddha. ◙ Country Life: Melantrichova 15; Map L4; 224 213366; **KK** • Dhaba Beas: Týnská 19; Map M3; 608 035727; **KK** • Little Buddha: Úvoz 46; Map A3; 220 513894; **KK**

Late-Night Eating
Unless you're willing to try the sausage stands on Wenceslas Square, finding a bite late at night will prove challenging. The club Zlatý Strom (see p77) serves food 24 hours a day. Better hotels have late-night room service.

Breakfast
Your hotel will probably include a Continental breakfast with the price of your room. While Irish fry-ups can be found at bars such as the James Joyce and Caffrey's, American diner-style breakfasts are largely unheard of. Cafés increasingly serve hemenex – ham and eggs – but seldom open before 9am. ◙ James Joyce: U obecního dvora 4; Map M2; 224 818851; **K** • Caffrey's: Staroměstské náměstí 10; Map M3; 224 828031; **KK**

Brunch
If you're travelling on a budget but still want a taste of the good life, you can see how the other half eat without breaking the bank by doing brunch at one of the city's fine-dining establishments. Brunch buffets, complete with champagne and jazz, abound and seldom cost more than Kč600.

Restaurant Classes
State-licensed eating establishments fall into one of three classes, with first class being the finest and three the plainest. The restaurant's class should be posted by the front door. These classifications are no indications of quality. A third-class pub may very well offer better food than a first-class restaurant at times.

For a guide to restaurant prices See p79

131

Left **Antiques shop** Right **Second-hand bookshop**

🔟 Shopping Tips

1 Credit Cards
The more expensive the item, the more likely it will be that you can pay for it with a credit card. Shops selling souvenirs are more likely to accept credit cards than those selling necessities. Cards accepted by an establishment will be indicated on the shop's front door.

2 VAT Refunds
Tourists are entitled to a refund of the value-added tax on purchases. Ask for a tax-free shopping cheque and tax-free envelope at the store. Complete the cheque and have it stamped at customs within 30 days. In Prague, visitors can collect their refund at several shops at Ruzyně airport *(see p126)*.

3 Baskets and Bags
If there are shopping carts or baskets at the front of the store, take one as you go in. It's common courtesy – shopkeepers will assume you're a shoplifter without one – and it helps regulate the number of shoppers in the often tiny stores. Bags for your purchases may cost extra.

4 Small Change
Prague shopkeepers demonstrate a disturbing antipathy towards mathematics and always appreciate it if you have exact change, down to the last crown. Don't be surprised if the shop

assistant fishes the correct coins out of your hand. Smaller shops may even refuse to accept banknotes larger than Kč1,000.

5 Specialist Shops
Large department stores such as Tesco have now introduced one-stop shopping, but there is still the tendency in Prague for shops to specialize to an amusing degree. A *papírnictví* sells everything made of paper, from notepads to sanitary napkins, while the only place you'll find an alarm clock is at a *hodinářství*.

6 Bargain Food
Whole loaves of fresh sourdough bread go for less than Kč20. But be warned – this bread does not contain any preservatives, so it starts to go off after a day. Shops selling *grilované kuře* (roast chicken) are dotted around the city. Order a quarter or half bird to eat there, or, if you are in self-catering accommodation, you can take a whole bird home for a great dinner.

7 Fresh Vegetables
Large supermarkets often trade in quality for quantity when it comes to produce. The best fruit and vegetables are found at various outdoor markets around Prague. In the city centre, try Havelská.

8 Antiques
Antiques dealers and junk merchants abound in the city centre. Going further afield will offer you an even better selection and prices. You may need a special permit to export antiques from the Czech Republic; ask the dealer. If you're looking for Soviet paraphernalia, be warned that anything you find these days is likely to be a replica.

9 Books
If you're looking for some reading material for the next leg of your journey, head to Big Ben or The Globe bookstore, but don't expect the latest titles. Or try Czech booksellers such as Kanzelsberger or Neoluxor, where English-language classics go for a song. 🅰 *Big Ben: Malá Štupartská 5; Map M3 • The Globe: Pštrossova 6; Map E5 • Kanzelsberger: Václavské náměstí 42; Map N5 • Neoluxor: Václavské náměstí 41; Map N5*

10 Bootleg Goods
As with most major cities, the odds are good that the Adidas trainers, Calvin Klein underwear or Umbro sportswear that you can buy on street stalls is not the real thing. Also be aware that many bazaars sell pirated CDs, videos and software, so the quality is likely to be dubious, if not downright unusable.

Establishments that accept credit cards most commonly accept Visa, MasterCard and American Express.

Streetsmart

Left **Museum tickets** Right **Palác Akropolis nightclub**

📖10 Prague on a Budget

1 City Public Transport

You can buy 30-minute, 90-minute, 24-hour and 3-day passes valid for unlimited use on Prague's metro, trams and buses, as well as train, boat and funicular services. Validate the ticket once and enjoy the ride. Ticket inspectors can levy a fine of Kč800–1,500 for tickets that have not been validated.

2 Opera

Prague opera continues to defy the laws of supply and demand. Even the best seats are cheap by western standards, but it's possible to buy standing-room only tickets and then slip into a seat in the largely empty hall when the overture begins.

3 Concerts

Corporate and state sponsorship keeps ticket prices – and musicians' salaries – low for the city's major orchestras. The Czech Radio Orchestra, Prague Symphony Orchestra and other ensembles regularly give masterful performances, the tickets to which are seldom more than a few hundred crowns.

4 Beer

There's rarely any need to pay more than Kč40 for a half-litre of draft beer. Even within the centre, Kč30 beer is not uncommon. Or journey out to Žižkov (see p116) or other working-class neighbourhoods for glasses as cheap as Kč12.

5 Food

Even less expensive than pub fare is the food served cafeteria-style at the city's many lunch counters and buffets. Grab a tray, your Czech dictionary and join the queue. Food is usually sold by weight. Lunch, with beer, should be less than Kč150.

6 Accommodation

Hostels usually have small double and even single rooms that offer greater privacy (see p144). Travellers can also find rooms or even entire flats for rent by the week (see p146). Check the bulletin boards at The Globe Bookstore (see p112) and Radost nightclub (see p111).

7 Travel in the Czech Republic

Students and teachers qualify for discounts on bus and train tickets, as well as airfares offered by GTS International. Czech trains have first- and second-class cabins, the latter being the cheaper. You can travel to most destinations within the Czech Republic and back for less than Kč700. ⊗ GTS International; Zikova 11 • 224 325235 • www.gtsint.cz

8 Free Prague Tours

This is a great way to explore Prague with a guide. Free Prague Tours is run by licenced English-speaking guides who are also history buffs and people orientated. Tipping the guide at the end, or whenever you choose to leave, is a way of showing appreciation and you will still save money. Meetings are daily in the Old Town Square at 11am and 2pm.

9 Clubbing

While admission to Karlovy Lázně, Radost FX and Roxy will cost you Kč100 or more at weekends, even these big clubs have free nights during the week. Smaller clubs further afield, such as Palác Akropolis, Music Club Červ and Industry 55, are cheaper and more intimate but a little less polished (see pp66–7).

10 Museums

Admission to National Gallery exhibitions is typically low, as is the fee to access the various National Museum buildings scattered around town. You may save even more money by purchasing a combined ticket, which is valid for three days. Every year, on the second Saturday in May, all museums are free – visit www.prazskamuzejninoc.cz for more details.

Left **Náměstí Republiky, starting point for guided bus tours** Right **Wallenstein Garden**

Prague for the Disabled

Public Transport
Prague is improving in terms of accessibility for the disabled. Most metro stations have lifts and auditory beacons for the blind, though the older ones in the centre remain largely inaccessible. Many trams and buses have specially lowered floors to enable easy access; visit www.dpp.cz for more information. The city's cobbled streets can be hard going.

Overcoming Barriers
This free brochure outlines four sightseeing routes, with easy-to-read maps and brief informative texts, for wheelchair-users. The guide also lists barrier-free galleries, monuments, restaurants, public bathrooms and shops along the route. Pick it up at the Prague Organization of Wheelchair Users.

Prague Organization of Wheelchair Users
In addition to publishing the above brochure, this group lobbies for the rights of the disabled. You can pick up the brochure and get advice about various other disability issues at their office near Náměstí Republiky. Some of their staff speak English. ⚘ *Prague Organization of Wheelchair Users: Benediktská 6 • Map N2 • 224 827210 • www.pov.cz*

Bus Routes
Two bus routes are dedicated to wheelchair-users and connect vast areas not reachable by metro or tram. Carrying passengers from far-flung housing developments to a few central locations, they're not much use to tourists. Many other buses have low platforms, but again, they mainly serve outlying areas.

Bus Tours
Those visitors who have trouble walking can get an overview of the city by taking an open-topped bus tour around town. Pre-recorded narration in several languages plays during the trip. Look for the buses on Old Town Square *(see pp14–17)* and Náměstí Republiky.

Accessible Sights
As may now be clear, Prague isn't the most disabled-friendly of the world's capitals. The following sights are partly accessible to wheelchair-users, although getting to them is sometimes a problem: St Vitus's Cathedral *(see pp12–13)*, the Old Royal Palace *(see pp8–11)*, the Old Town Hall *(see pp16–17)*, the National Theatre *(see p64)*, Wallenstein Garden *(see p40)*, Franciscan Garden *(see p105)*, the Municipal House *(see p73)*, the Church of St James *(see p74)* and the Estates Theatre *(see p65)*.

Discounted Tickets
Hearing impaired visitors will be happy to learn that most sights offer discounted entry.

Hotels
Most of the newer hotels are accessible to wheelchair-users, although the number of barrier-free rooms is small. Hats off to the Hilton, where there are no fewer than 15 barrier-free rooms *(see p139)*. The Prague Organization of Wheelchair Users will also be able to supply a list of accessible places to stay.

Helper Dogs
Canine assistants to the visually impaired are permitted in banks, official buildings and historic monuments as well as on public transport. Be aware that not all members of Prague's thriving dog population are as well-trained – avoiding dog mess is a problem for the sighted too.

Other Resources
Other organizations in the city that are a good source of information for disabled travellers are listed below. ⚘ *Czech Union of the Disabled: Karlinské Náměstí 12; 222 317489 • Czech Blind United: Krakovská 21; Map G5; 221 462462; www.sons.cz • Accessible Prague: www.accessible prague.com*

Left **Goethe Institute** Right **Charles University**

🔟 Studying in Prague

Czech Lessons
Large language schools like SF Servis offer Czech lessons for foreigners, as does Charles University. Their packages include three-week summer courses for about Kč15,000. ◈ *SFF Servis Plus: Kaprova 42/14 • Map K3 • 226 220069*
• *sffservisplus.cz*

Goethe Institute
Accomplished German speakers can study Kafka in the original language; the rest can brush up their language skills or start from scratch. A three-month course in conversational German costs Kč5,000. ◈ *Goethe-Institut Prag: Masarykovo nábřeži 32 • Map E5 • 221 962111* • *www.goethe.de*

French Institute
English may have replaced it as the lingua franca, so to speak, but French is still useful for travellers. Four-month courses for beginners cost around Kč4,000. You can also study French art, history, literature – even creative writing. ◈ *Institut Francais de Prague: Štepánská 35 • Map F5 • 221 401011 • www.ifp.cz*

Anglo-American University
This liberal arts college offers internationally accredited degrees in business administration, international relations, diplomacy, law, humanities and social sciences. All courses are taught in English. ◈ *Anglo-American College: Lázeňská 4 • Map D3 • 257 530202* • *www.aauni.edu*

Charles University
The oldest university in Central Europe offers some courses in English in its many degree and non-degree programmes. Short-term courses are taught over the summer months. ◈ *Univerzita Karlova v Praze: Albertov 7/32 • Map B6 • 224 990420 • www.ujop.cuni.cz*

New York University
New York University offers study-abroad programmes for students enrolled at its US campuses and at affiliated universities elsewhere. Students enrolled in Czech universities may audit classes. ◈ *New York University in Prague: Malé náměstí 2 • Map L4 • 224 226658 • www.nyu.cz*

Prague Film School
One of Europe's leading film schools, providing practical training in the main disciplines of filmmaking. With its world-class facilities and international faculty, the school draws students from all over the world. Around 400 films are shot here annually. Every student is involved in up to 30 productions every year, many of which are featured in top film festivals. ◈ *Pštrossova 19 • Map E5 • 257 534013* • *www.filmstudies.cz*

International TEFL Certificate
This private firm has been training its students all over the world for six years to teach English to foreigners. Courses last four weeks. ITC assists graduates in job placement worldwide. ◈ *www.itc-training.com*

English-Language Grammar Schools
Expat parents can enrol their children at the International School of Prague, Riverside School and other grammar schools offering English-language instruction for children aged 3–19. ◈ *International School of Prague: www.isp.cz* • *Riverside School: www.riversideschool.cz*

Driving Lessons
Long-term residents will need to apply for a Czech driving licence. Some driving schools such as Autoškola Ing. Ondšej Horázny and Autoškola Dejvice offer instruction and testing in English. See the Prague *Yellow Pages* for a more complete list. ◈ *Autoškola Dejvice: www.autoskoladejvice.cz* • *Autoškola Ing. Ondřej Horázny: www.horazny.cz*

Left **Bureau de Change sign** Centre **Post Office sign** Right **Prague bank**

🔟 Banking and Communications

1 Currency
The Czech Republic's currency is the crown (Kč). Crown notes come in denominations of Kč5,000, Kč2,000, Kč1,000, Kč500, Kč200, Kč100 and the increasingly rare Kč50. Coins come in the following denominations: Kč1, Kč2, Kč5, Kč10, Kč20 and Kč50.

2 Banks
Most banks are open from 8am to 5 or 6pm. Although some banks are worth visiting just for their stunning interiors, such as ex-Živnostenská banka building, the only other reason you'll need to go to a Prague bank is if you want to take advantage of the typically lower fees they charge for currency exchange.
🔍 *Unicredit bank: Na Příkopě 20 • Map P4*

3 Exchange
Although they may advertise "0 per cent commission", all bureaux de change will take a cut. The conversion rates vary little from exchange to exchange so there's little point shopping around. Note that very few will accept coins. It's a good idea to convert your crowns back to your own currency before you leave, as the Czech currency has a very low value outside of the country itself.

4 ATMs
Bankomats are widely available throughout the city centre. The machines recognize major credit cards and global banking systems such as Cirrus. As with all cities worldwide, be vigilant when making use of ATMs after dark.

5 Credit Cards and Travellers' Cheques
Major credit cards are widely accepted at shops and restaurants that cater to tourists, but always check on your way in. Travellers' cheques, on the other hand, are seldom accepted, although American Express cashes and sells their cheques at their various offices across the city.

6 Telephones
When not out of order, payphones accept either coins or phone cards *(telefonní karty)*, available at post offices and newsagents. More than 70 per cent of Czechs have mobile phones. You can rent a mobile phone at Prague's Ruzyně airport *(see p126)*.

7 Post
The main post office is lovely inside and worth a visit, whether or not you need to mail a postcard or letter overseas. It also offers a telegram service and a large phone room, which is a good way of making overseas telephone calls.
🔍 *Main Post Office: Jindřišská 14 • Map P6 • 221 131111*

8 Internet
As in most cities, nowadays one can find an Internet café on almost every corner. Expect to be charged upwards of Kč60 an hour, with a minimum time of 15 minutes. Many visitors do their surfing at The Globe. 🔍 *The Globe: Pštrossova 6 • Map E5 • 224 934203*

9 Newspapers and Magazines
In addition to the locally produced *Prague Tribune* and *The Prague Post* (see p128), downtown newsstands carry US weeklies like *Time* as well as international newspapers such as *The Guardian, Wall Street Journal* and the *International Herald Tribune*.

🔟 Television and Radio
You'll find some English-language broadcasts on the BBC at 101.1 FM, as well as an abundance of Czech and Slovak. If your hotel has satellite hook-ups, expect the usual fare of Sky and MTV. Public Czech Television often broadcasts classic films in English with Czech subtitles.

Left **Beware of pickpockets on Prague buses** Centre **Police sign** Right **Pharmacy sign**

🔟 Security and Health

1 Emergency Numbers

To call an ambulance, dial 155; for police, 158. In the event of a fire, call 150. Speak slowly and calmly so the operator can understand you. For an English-speaking emergency operator, dial 112. You may also wish to carry your embassy's phone number with you.

2 Police

Prague's municipal police are generally helpful to (law-abiding) visitors, although they continue to be dogged with accusations of bribe-taking. Don't confuse members of private security services and Prague Castle guards for state or municipal police officers.

3 Hospitals

Prague's doctors increasingly speak English and are accustomed to western standards of care. Some private clinics that cater to foreigners, such as the Canadian Medical Centre, have doctors on call 24 hours a day. Should you need in-patient care, go to the foreigners' clinic at Na Homolce Hospital. ⊗ *Canadian Medical Centre: Veleslavínská 1; 724 300301* • *Na Homolce Hospital: Roentgenova 2; 257 272144*

4 Fire

If you need to report a fire, dial 150 and tell the operator what is burning

and where. In the street, it's not uncommon to see a smouldering waste bin, where someone has carelessly thrown a lit cigarette. Don't worry – someone will be along in a minute with a bucket of water to put it out.

5 Dentists

Czech dental care is considered among the best in Europe. For emergencies, call 224 946981. For routine care, try the English-speaking dentists at Elite Dental Prague or Millennium Dental Care. ⊗ *Elite Dental Prague: Vodičkova 5; 222 510888; www. elitedental.cz* • *Millennium Dental Care: V Celnicí 10; 221 033405; www.mdc.cz*

6 Pharmacies

For even such common medicines as aspirin or cold remedies, you'll need to visit a *lékárna*. At weekends you can use pharmacies in shopping centres and galleries throughout Prague. Several central pharmacies operate 24 hours a day. ⊗ *Palackého 5; Map F4; 224 946982* • *Štefánikova 6; 257 320918* • *Belgická 37; Map H6; 222 513396*

7 Precautions

Consult a physician before your trip and check whether your health insurance covers you abroad. If it doesn't, be sure to take out extra insurance to avoid high

charges should you fall ill. Also be aware that your medication may be known by a different name brand abroad. Your doctor may also recommend an inoculation against hepatitis before your trip, although this isn't strictly necessary.

8 Pickpockets

Pickpockets target tourists in crowded spaces where they can jostle you. Distribute your valuables among several inside pockets and never carry more cash than you need. Leave photocopies of your passport in your hotel room.

9 Food and Water Safety

The fat-heavy Czech diet may cause indigestion, so bring along your favourite stomach-settler. Tap water is safe to drink, but even local residents prefer bottled water. The most dangerous fluid in a city full of bars is alcohol; watch your intake – Czech beer is stronger than a lot of other varieties.

10 Smoking

Second-hand smoke is a fact of life in Prague. Smoke-free restaurants and cafés are rare. If cigarettes aggravate your health or enjoyment, be sure to visit in summer, when you can spend more time outside and breathe in fresher air.

Left **Hotel Hoffmeister** Right **Hotel Paříž**

🔟 Luxury Hotels

Hotel Hoffmeister
The Hoffmeister is a quiet, modern hotel in the shadow of Prague Castle, celebrated for its gourmet restaurant and gallery of caricatures by the owner's father. The rooms are sumptuously and uniquely furnished. ⊗ *Pod Bruskou 7 • Map D1 • 251 017111 • www. hoffmeister.cz* • **KK**

U Zlaté studně
Once owned by astronomer Tycho de Brahe, the hotel "at the Golden Well" adjoins the Ledeburg Gardens, offering unparalleled views. All rooms have whirlpool baths and Richelieu furniture. Book well in advance. ⊗ *U Zlaté studně 4 • Map C2 • 257 011213 • www. zlatastudna.cz; www. goldenwell.cz* • **KKKKK**

Hotel U krále Karla
Formerly a Benedictine monastery, the King Charles Hotel was popular in the 16th century for the reputed healing powers of its well. The hotel is a blissful matrimony of Baroque furnishings and modern luxuries. ⊗ *Úvoz 4 • Map B2 • 257 533594 • www. ukralekarla.cz • No air conditioning* • **KKK**

Hotel Pod věží
The "Hotel Under the Tower" guards the Malá Strana end of Charles

Bridge. The rooms are graciously outfitted with period furniture and comfortable reproductions. Hair-stylists, barbers, manicurists and masseuses are on call. ⊗ *Mostecká 2 • Map D3 • 257 532041 • www.podvezi.com* • **KK**

Four Seasons
Swaddled in the Four Seasons trademark luxury, guests may forget where they are. A quick stroll on the riverside terrace should remind them. The restaurant Allegro is one of Prague's best. Top-notch, all round. ⊗ *Veleslavínova 2a • Map K3 • 221 427000 • www. fourseasons.com • Dis. access* • **KKKKK**

Grand Hotel Bohemia
Old European decorum meets Old European decadence: built in 1920, the Bohemia was home to one of Jazz-Age Prague's liveliest clubs. Its 78 rooms were refurbished in 2002. The best views are from the eighth floor. ⊗ *Králodvorská 4 • Map P3 • 234 608111 • www. grandhotelbohemia.cz • Dis. access* • **KKKK**

Archibald at the Charles Bridge
Also known by its address Na Kampě 15, the "House at Charles Bridge" is close enough to the river that guests can hear the Vltava rushing over the weir.

The rooms and suites are warmly furnished in a country style. ⊗ *Na Kampě 15 • Map D3 • 234 652800 • www. archibald.cz* • **KKK**

Mandarin Oriental
The hotel is located in a restored Dominican monastery. Its spa is in the former chapel and several of its 99 rooms have views over the city to Prague Castle. ⊗ *Nebovidská 1 • Map C3 • 233 088888 • www. mandarinoriental.com/ prague* • **KKKKK**

Hotel Paříž
Built in 1904, this Art Nouveau treasure retains all its original charm while incorporating modern conveniences like heated bathroom floors and king-size beds in all rooms. The Royal Tower Suite has a spectacular 360-degree view. ⊗ *U Obecního domu 1 • Map P3 • 222 195666 • www.hotel-pariz.cz* • **KKKKK**

Pachtův Palace
Rooms at the Pachtuv Palace are luxuriously over the top, with painted ceilings and medieval decor, fittings and fixtures. Located on the waterfront, the views are spectacular. It is so romantic that it may be hard to leave your room. ⊗ *Karoliny Světlé 34 • Map K6 • 234 705111; 00800 77477477 (UK) • www. mamaison.com* • **KKKK**

  Note: *Unless otherwise stated, all hotels accept credit cards, and have en-suite bathrooms and air conditioning.*

Above **Holiday Inn**

Price Categories

For a standard,	**K** under Kč1,500
double room per	**KK** Kč1,500–Kč3,000
night (with breakfast	**KKK** Kč3,000–Kč4,500
if included), taxes	**KKKK** Kč4,500–Kč6,000
and extra charges.	**KKKKK** over Kč6,000

░10 Chain Hotels

Hotel Ibis
A no-nonsense hotel with modern amenities and a devotion to customer service. The rooms are small, clean and comfortable. A good choice for travellers who don't want to spend a lot of time sitting around. 🅂 *Plzeňská 14, Smíchov* • *221 701700* • *www. hotelibis.cz* • *Dis. access* • **KK**

Novotel
With underground parking, a small gym and swimming pool, piano bar and Cote Jardin restaurant, the Novotel offers a budget version of luxury. Children under 16 stay free. 🅂 *Kateřinská 38* • *221 104999* • *www.novotel. com* • *Dis. access* • **KKKK**

Holiday Inn
The Holiday Inn adjoins the Congress Centre near Vyšehrad. Drivers will appreciate the large garage and adjoining petrol station. Ask for a castle view. 🅂 *Na Pankráci 15* • *Map B6* • *296 895000* • *www.holidayinn.cz* • *Dis. access* • **KK**

Hotel Best Western Meteor Plaza
Medieval travellers who found city gates closed for the night stayed at a much earlier hotel on this spot. The fitness centre on the premises has two whirlpool baths. For a longer stay, book room No. 510. 🅂 *Hybernská 6* • *Map P4* • *224 192111* • *www.hotel-meteor.cz* • **KKKK**

Prague Marriott
Bright and welcoming, with pleasant touches such as complimentary newspapers, signs in Braille and rooms with lofts (great for families). All rooms have Internet access and 24-hour room service. 🅂 *V Celnici 8* • *Map G2* • *222 888888* • *www.marriottprague. com* • *Dis. access* • **KKKK**

Hilton
Prague's premiere convention hotel boasts nearly 800 rooms and suites, an extensive fitness centre, a casino and the largest meeting facilities aside from the Congress Centre in Vyšehrad. Rates go down in summer. 🅂 *Pobřežní 1* • *Map H1* • *224 841111* • *www.hilton.com* • *Dis. access* • **KKKK**

Hilton Prague Old Town
Situated between Masarykovo nádraží and the Old Town, the hotel offers a fitness centre with pool, three restaurants and 305 rooms; all rooms have satellite TV and voice mail. 🅂 *V Celnici 7* • *Map G2* • *222 822220* • *www. hiltonpragueoldtown.com* • *Dis. access* • **KKKK**

Kempinski
Once the Baroque Palace U Věžníků, this hotel offers an appealing blend of the historical and contemporary throughout. The rooms are large and comfortable. Suites and palace studios are also available. Amenities include a spa and wellness centre, and conference rooms. 🅂 *Hybernská 12* • *Map G3* • *226 226111* • *www. kempinski.com* • *Dis. access* • **KKKKK**

Radisson BLU Alcron
In the 1930s, the Alcron was Prague's answer to New York's Ritz. The Radisson hotel group has carefully revived the hotel's Art Nouveau dandiness, besmirched by 40 years of secret police surveillance. There are two excellent restaurants on site. 🅂 *Štěpánská 40* • *Map F5* • *222 820000* • *www. radissonblu.com/hotel-prague* • *Dis. access* • **KKKKK**

Fortuna West
Located well outside the centre, the Comfort is nearer Ruzyně airport *(see p126)* than downtown. There are 159 basic but clean rooms, all with satellite TV, and there's a useful on-site car park and conference facilities. 🅂 *Mrkvičkova 2, Prague 5* • *234 712401* • *www. hotelfortunawestprague.com* • *No air conditioning* • **K**

Left **Hotel Metamorphis** Right **Hotel Ungelt**

Old Town Hotels

Casa Marcello
Casa Marcello's elegantly appointed rooms embrace their 13th-century character; wandering the hotel's many stairs and hallways, you'll think you're in an Escher print. There is a small fitness club and excellent restaurant on the premises.
✆ *Řásnovka 783 • Map N1 • 222 311230 • www. casa-marcello.cz • **KK***

Inter-Continental
The Inter-Continental pulls out all the stops for its Club-Level guests, but all visitors will feel pampered. The large fitness centre has exercise machines, a swimming pool and a spa. On a budget? Rooms with city views are less expensive than those overlooking the Vltava. ✆ *Pařížská 30 • Map E1 • 296 631111 • www.ichotelsgroup.com • **KKKK***

Lippert
Across the street from Franz Kafka's birthplace, with unobstructed views of St Nicholas and Týn churches, the Black Fox building is listed as a UNESCO World Cultural Heritage Site. There are more graceful places to stay, but few as well situated. There are only 12 rooms available, so book well in advance.
✆ *Mikulášská 2 • Map M3 • 224 232250 • www. hotel-lippert.cz • **KKK***

Hotel Aurus
You'll tell the folks back home about this one. Located in the heart of Prague, this family-run four-star property is one of the most beautiful historical monuments protected by UNESCO. Old Town Square and Charles Bridge are only a short walk away.
✆ *Karlova 3 • Map K5 • 222 220262 • www. aurushotel.cz • **KKK***

Hotel Metamorphis
Stylish touches like parquet floors, tiled stoves and stirring views of Ungelt coutyard and the intricate façade of St James set the Metamorphis apart. No lift. The patio restaurant does big business in summer.
✆ *Malá Štupartská 5 • Map N3 • 221 771011 • www. metamorphis.cz • **KKKKK***

U Medvídků
An excellent location, not only is the *pension* at the Bears centrally located, it's close to tram and metro stations, and situated above the city's favourite Budvar pub.
✆ *Na Perštýně 7 • Map L6 • info@umedvidku.cz • www.umedvidku.cz • No air conditioning • **KK***

Hotel Ungelt
The immediate vicinity is haunted by at least two ghosts, but guests at the Ungelt have registered no complaints. Perhaps they're sleeping too soundly in the nine renovated 10th-century apartments to notice. The courtyard offers glimpses of Týn Church. Book early. ✆ *Štupartská 7 • Map N3 • 221 771011 • www.ungelt.cz • No air conditioning • **KKKK***

Hotel Clementin
The Clementin has the peculiar honour of being the narrowest building in the city. As you might expect, the nine rooms in this Gothic building are small, but gracious. You might have trouble with large luggage.
✆ *Seminářská 4 • Map K4 • 222 231520 • www. clementin.cz • **KKK***

Hotel U staré paní
A no-frills affair, but the clean, modern building is staffed with an amiable crew. Each of the 18 rooms has a minibar and satellite TV, but for better entertainment, catch the acts at the club downstairs.
✆ *Michalská 9 • Map L5 • 224 228090 • www. ustarepani.cz • No air conditioning • **KK***

Hotel Josef
Modern and trendy in design, Hotel Josef fits in with Prague's new urban chic image with its simple clean-cut interiors and spacious rooms.
✆ *Rybná 20 • Map N2 • 221 700111 • www. hoteljosef.com • **KKK***

***Note:** Unless otherwise stated, all hotels accept credit cards, and have en-suite bathrooms and air conditioning*

ČERTOVKA HOTEL

Above **Hotel Čertovka**

TOP 10 Malá Strana and Hradčany Hotels

1 U Tří Pštrosů
The hotel at the Three Ostriches gets its name from a 16th-century owner who was a purveyor of ostrich feathers. The rooms are comfortably furnished and extremely quiet considering their proximity to Charles Bridge.
◈ Dražického náměstí 12 • Map D3 • 777 876667 • www.utripstrosu.cz • No air conditioning • **KKK**

2 Rezidence Lundborg
In case the view of the Charles Bridge isn't enough, each of the 13 suites is equipped with a computer with free Internet access and a Jacuzzi. In the cellar, you'll find the foundations of the Judith Bridge. ◈ U lužického semináře 3 • Map D2 • 257 011911 • www.lundborg.se • **KKKK**

3 Hotel Čertovka
You can watch small boats pass beneath Charles Bridge on the Čertovka canal from windows overlooking Prague's "Little Venice". Top floor rooms have views of the castle. Parking is some distance from the hotel. ◈ U lužického semináře 2 • Map D2 • 257 011500 • www.certovka.cz • No air conditioning • **KKK**

4 Hotel Sax
Tucked into the heart of Malá Strana, the modern Sax is close to the Church of St Nicholas, the Church of Our Lady Victorious and Prague Castle. The 19 rooms and three suites surround a bright central atrium. ◈ Jánský vršek 3 • Map B3 • 257 531268 • www.sax.cz • **KKK**

5 Hotel Waldstein
Adjoining Duke Albrecht von Wallenstein's palace on a quiet courtyard, this cosy hotel features 15 rooms and 10 suites. All the rooms are very comfortable and are furnished with antiques and repro-ductions. ◈ Valdštejnske náměstí 6 • Map C2 • 257 533938 • www.hotelwaldstein.cz • No air conditioning • **KKK**

6 Zlatá Hvězda
Built in 1372 as the residence of Hradčany's mayor, the Golden Star has a long history of elegance. The rooms and apartments are decked out with period furniture and modern baths. Room No. 33 is sublime.
◈ Nerudova 48 • Map C2 • 257 532867 • www.hotelgoldenstar.cz • No air conditioning • **KKK**

7 Biskupský dům
The Bishop's House actually occupies two buildings: one is the Prague bishop's former residence; the other was a butcher's in the 18th century. Between them are 45 rooms, all com-fortable and tastefully furnished. ◈ Dražického náměstí 6 • Map D3 • 257 532320 • www.hotelbishopshouse.cz • No air conditioning • Dis. access • **KKK**

8 Dům U Červeného Lva
From the House at the Red Lion, guests can see either Prague Castle and Nerudova or Petřín Hill to the south. Guests will find it hard to leave room No. 32. ◈ Nerudova 41 • Map C2 • 257 533832 • www.hotelredlion.cz • No air conditioning • **K**

9 Domus Henrici
Built in 1372 on the steep hill overlooking the city, this small hotel is a stone's throw from Prague Castle. Each of the eight rooms has views of Petřín Hill and thoughtful amenities such as rocking chairs. ◈ Loretánská 11 • Map B2 • 220 511369 • www.domus-henrici.cz • No air conditioning • **KKK**

10 Aria
An unusual little hotel, where each of the rooms, though not large, are modelled to a particular musical legend, be it Dizzy Gillespie or Mozart. The hotel's musical director will also advise you on concerts you can attend. ◈ Tržiště 9 • Map C2 • 225 334111 • www.ariahotel.net • **KKKKK**

Left **Doorman, Hotel Palace** Right **Hotel Evropa**

TOP 10 New Town Hotels

1 Hotel Palace
As classy as the hotels around the corner on Wenceslas Square, the Palace is renowned for its excellent service. The hotel offers several packages, including a two-day honeymoon deal, complete with tours and other extras. Little luxuries include marble-lined bathrooms. ⊗ *Panská 12 • Map N5 • 224 093111 • www. palacehotel.cz • Dis. access* • **KKK**

2 Hotel Jalta
This Wenceslas Square designer hotel offers 89 stylish rooms and five luxurious suites. The Como restaurant serves excellent Mediterranean cuisine. Other amenities include a casino, a fitness centre and business centre. ⊗ *Václavské náměstí 45 • Map N6 • 222 822111 • www.hoteljalta.cz • Dis. access* • **KKK**

3 Hotel 16 U Sv. Kateřiny
The rooms and apartments at St Catherine's luxuriously furnished hotel are great value. Located near the Prague Botanical Gardens and the river, the family-run inn is very quiet and has little eccentricities like the display of lovely junk from the bazaar next door. ⊗ *Kateřinská 16 • Map F6 • 224 919676 • www.hotel16.cz • Dis. access* • **KK**

4 Art Deco Imperial Hotel
This hotel offers accommodation aimed at leisure and business travellers who prefer the intimacy and individual approach of a boutique hotel. Modern technology and comforts combine seamlessly with the original Art Deco interiors. ⊗ *Na Poříčí 15 • Map G2 • 246 011600 • www.hotel-imperial.cz* • **KKKK**

5 Hotel Adria
In the 14th century, Carmelite nuns serving at the Church of Our Lady of the Snows had their convent on this site. The 89 snug rooms look out on either the Franciscan Gardens or busy Wenceslas Square, with its many shops, cinemas and cafés. Guarded parking nearby. ⊗ *Václavské náměstí 26 • Map N6 • 221 081111 • www.adria.cz • Dis. access* • **KKK**

6 Hotel Opera
The rooms at the Hotel Opera are more low key than the hot-pink Neo-Renaissance façade. They are great value for money, bright and comfortable. Particularly charming are No. 107, with its Mucha prints and pink velvet daybed, and the corner room No. 106, with its large bath. ⊗ *Těšnov 13 • Map H1 • 222 315609 • www.hotel-opera.cz* • **KKK**

7 Hotel Evropa
Despite the Art Nouveau façade and café, guests may miss modern conveniences; not all rooms have en-suite bathrooms. The interior is somewhat outdated but first- and second-floor rooms have good views over Wenceslas Square. ⊗ *Václavské náměstí 25 • Map P6 • 224 228215 • www.evropahotel.cz • No air conditioning* • **KK**

8 Novoměstský Hotel
A bit old fashioned, but the staff are helpful. Close to Karlovo náměstí and the New Town Hall. ⊗ *Řeznická 4 • Map F5 • 221 419911 • www. novomestskyhotel.cz • No air conditioning* • **KKK**

9 Hotel Icon
This boutique hotel offers natural handmade beds from Sweden in every room. An oriental massage centre enhances its chic image. ⊗ *V jámě 6 • Map F4 • 221 634100 • www. iconhotel.eu* • **KKK**

10 Hotel Jungmann
This charming hotel is situated close to Wenceslas Square and other sights of interest, in one of the narrowest houses in Prague. It has eight rooms, four with double beds. ⊗ *Jungmannovo náměstí 2 • 224 219501 • www. antikhotels.com* • **KKK**

 Note: *Unless otherwise stated, all hotels accept credit cards, and have en-suite bathrooms and air conditioning*

Price Categories

For a standard,
double room per
night (with breakfast
if included), taxes
and extra charges.

K	under Kč1,500
KK	Kč1,500–Kč3,000
KKK	Kč3,000–Kč4,500
KKKK	Kč4,500–Kč6,000
KKKKK	over Kč6,000

Above **Botel Albatros**

🔟 Novelty Hotels

1 Hotel Amadeus
Affordable three-star accommodation near Prague city centre, Amadeus offers spacious rooms and apartments suitable for families and business travellers. Pets are welcome too. 🅢 *Dalimilova 10, Žižkov* • *Map B6* • *224 238150* • *www.hotelkafka.cz* • *No air conditioning* • **KK**

2 Botel Racek
Floating on the Vltava's right bank, near the local yacht club and the city's large swimming and sports entertainment area at Žluté Lázně, the Racek offers 81 cabins, a restaurant and a top-deck disco. Nearby trams will take you to the centre in 10 minutes. 🅢 *Podolské nábřeží, Podolí* • *241 431628* • *www.botelracek. eu* • *No air conditioning* • **K**

3 Botel Albatros
The Albatros fancies itself romantic; enjoying a drink on the deck, gazing at Prague Castle you'd be inclined to agree. Old Town Square is a 10-minute walk away. The cabins are small, as befits a boat, but cosy. 🅢 *Nábřeží Ludvíka Svobody* • *224 810547* • *www.botelalbatros.cz* • *No air conditioning* • **KK**

4 Botel Admiral
Moored across the river from Palackého náměstí and the modern spires of Emmaus Monastery, the Admiral offers 82 tiny cabins. Travellers who prefer more space should book one of the four apartments. Restaurant and night club at the Terrace. 🅢 *Hořejší nábřeží, Smíchov* • *Map A6* • *257 321302* • *www.admiral-botel.cz* • *No air conditioning* • **KKK**

5 Hotel Cloister Inn
The Jesuits founded the cloister that gives the hotel its name in the Middle Ages. The monastery complex was then occupied by the Grey Sisters of St Francis, who were in turn replaced by the secret police. The 75 rooms have modern amenities. 🅢 *Konviktská 14* • *Map K6* • *224 211020* • *www.cloister-inn.com* • **KK**

6 Hotel Expo'
Near Stromovka park, the Expo' was built to accommodate visitors attending trade fairs at the adjacent exhibition grounds. The 106 rooms each have satellite TV, Wi-Fi and minibar. 🅢 *Za elektrárnou 3, Holešovice* • *Map B5* • *266 712470* • *www.expoprag.cz* • *Dis. access* • **KK**

7 Orea Hotel Pyramida
This large hotel near Prague Castle resembles an Aztec pyramid. Trams stopping outside whisk guests along a scenic route to the city centre in minutes. There's a large fitness centre and a swimming pool. 🅢 *Bělohorská 24* • *Map B2* • *261 304577* • *www. hotelpyramida.cz* • *Dis. access* • **K**

8 Hotel Duo
This four-star hotel boasts excellent service and a contemporary experience for Prague's business and leisure guests. The hotel has a swimming pool, a beauty salon and an Internet café. 🅢 *Teplická 492, Praha 9* • *Map B6* • *266 131111* • *www.hotelduo.cz* • **KK**

9 Hotel Yasmin
This hotel has been designed with luxury in mind, with 196 rooms over seven floors. Tasteful furnishings adorn each of the rooms, and a 70s-retro globe hangs in the lobby. A summer terrace and the light airy feel offer a distinct difference from nearby offerings. 🅢 *Politických vězňů 12* • *Map P6* • *234 100100* • *www.hotel-yasmin. cz* • **KKK**

10 Little House in Střešovice
Situated in a country setting just a 15-minute walk from Prague Castle. The attic bedroom is furnished with antiques. Available only from March to November. Minimum three-night stay. 🅢 *Pod novým lesem 23, Střešovice* • *233 920118* • *stresovice@hprg. cz* • *No air conditioning* • **KK**

Left **Hostel ELF** Right **Hostel Advantage**

🔟 Hostels

Hostel Sokol
This central Malá Strana hostel takes its name from a First Republic national fitness movement. The six doubles and eight 12-bed rooms are up a suitably athletic flight of stairs. No smoking. ⊗ *Nosticova 2a • Map D3 • 257 007397 • www. hostelsokol.cz • No air conditioning • K*

Travellers' Hostel
This company has more than 25 years' experience hosting wanderers in a network of hostels. This Old Town hostel is above the Roxy nightclub, but keep your carousing to a minimum, since you share the building with anxious neighbours. Other locations around town are open during the summer. ⊗ *Dlouhá 33 • Map M2 • 224 826662 • www.travellers.cz • No air conditioning • KK*

Chili Hostel
This inexpensive hostel is located close to the Vltava River and the National Theatre. It provides rooms for individual backpackers, schools, large tour groups, couples and families. Facilities include a fully equipped kitchen and free Internet, as well as a room for parties in the basement. ⊗ *Pštrossova 7/205 • Map E5 • 603 119113 • www. chili.dj • K*

Sir Toby's Hostel
The staff here go to great lengths to be hospitable, throwing the occasional barbecue and helping travellers find other accommodation when the hostel is full. The bedrooms, baths and kitchen are immaculate. ⊗ *Dělnická 24, Holešovice • Map B5 • 246 032610 • www.sirtobys.com • Dis. access • No air conditioning • K*

Boathouse Hostel
Located 20 minutes south of the centre and run by strict rules, the Boathouse is not a party hostel. It does, however, offer numerous services, such as laundry, Internet access and bicycle and boat rental. Three to nine beds to a room. ⊗ *Lodnická 1 • 241 770051 • www.hostelboathouse. com • No air conditioning • No credit cards • K*

Old Prague Hostel
Located in the centre of Prague, this hostel has two- to five-bed rooms as well as four- to eight-bed dorms, some with private showers. There's also a fully equipped kitchen and dining room, Internet access and a movie lounge. ⊗ *Benediktská 2 • Map N2 • 224 829058 • www.oldpraguehostel.com • No air conditioning • K*

Miss Sophie's
Located just a stone's throw from the centre, this is an ideal base from which to explore the city. It offers dorms as well as private rooms with en suite bathrooms. Slightly more expensive are the apartments, complete with kitchen. ⊗ *Melounova 3 • Map G6 • 246 032621 • www.miss-sophies.com • No air conditioning • No credit cards • KK*

Hostel ELF
On the second floor of a *fin de siècle* building near the main bus and train stations, Hostel ELF's rooms range from singles to 11-bed dormitories. There is a shared kitchen, common room and garden. The staff will arrange walking tours for you. ⊗ *Husitská 11 • Map H3 • 222 540963 • www. hostelelf.com • No credit cards • No air conditioning • KK*

Hostel Advantage
Accommodation ranges from singles to seven-bed rooms. Kitchenette and TV, free Wi-Fi and two PCs are close to the reception desk. ⊗ *Sokolská 11 • Map G5 • 224 914062 • www.advantagehostel.cz • No air conditioning • KK*

Hostel Strahov
The dormitories are student housing through the school year, although Block 12 is always open. ⊗ *Vaníčkova 5, Strahov • Map A4 • 234 678111 • recepce@suz.cvut.cz • No air conditioning • K*

Price Categories

For a standard, double room per night (with breakfast if included), taxes and extra charges.

K	under Kč1,500
KK	Kč1,500–Kč3,000
KKK	Kč3,000–Kč4,500
KKKK	Kč4,500–Kč6,000
KKKKK	over Kč6,000

Above left **Pension Cora** Right **Pension Denisa**

Pensions and Bed-and-Breakfasts

1 U Raka

Prague's most romantic address, the House at the Crayfish started out as a barn in 1739. Inside the log walls are charming country-style rooms. Room No. 6 has its own garden, fireplace and well. Near Prague Castle and the Loreto. No children under 12. ✆ *Černínská 10 • Map A2 • 220 511100 • www. romantikhotel-uraka.cz* • **KK**

2 Pension Dientzenhofer

The quiet house on the banks of the Čertovka canal is the birthplace of architect Kilian Ignaz Dientzenhofer, who built the nearby Church of St Nicholas and other Baroque edifices. The garden is idyllic. ✆ *Nosticova 2 • Map D3 • 257 311319 • www. dientzenhofer.cz • Dis. access* • **KK**

3 Residence Liliová

Just around the corner from Charles Bridge, this lovely guesthouse in a historic building provides a quiet and comfortable place to stay. ✆ *Liliová 18 • Map K5 • 226 808200 • www. hotelliliovaprague.com • No air conditioning* • **KKK**

4 Pension Vyšehrad

This lovely guesthouse is nearly inside the Vyšehrad walls. Stroll through the park each evening at sunset or sit in the pension's stunning garden. The five

rooms are simply and comfortably furnished. Good access to public transport. Pets stay free. ✆ *Krokova 6 • Map B6 • 241 408455 • www. pension-vysehrad.cz • No air conditioning* • **KK**

5 Pension Cora

Located in a peaceful villa-quarter in southeast Prague, the Cora is not central, but nearby buses and the pension's cars can take you anywhere you need to go. Amenities include satellite TV and a billiard room. The hosts serve a big breakfast. ✆ *Ve Studeném 7a, Braník • 733 226342 • www.corahotel.cz • No air conditioning* • **K**

6 Pension Denisa

Reconstructed to high standards, the Denisa sits in a quiet neighbourhood just steps from the metro. The 43 rooms each have refrigerator and satellite TV; plus, your hosts bring breakfast to your room. ✆ *Národní obrany 33, Dejvice • Map A5 • 224 318969 • www.hotel-denisa.cz • No air conditioning* • **KK**

7 Church Pension

The Evangelic Church of the Czech Brethren has put its hospitality skills to the test at this small guesthouse. The rooms are suitably austere; not all have en-suite baths. Being a Christian guesthouse, you may encounter a

prayer group in the common room. The hosts are very pleasant. ✆ *Jungmannova 9 • Map M6 • 603 554785 or 296 245432 • www.church pension.cz • No air conditioning* • **KK**

8 Čelakovskeho sady

Overlooking the small green surrounding the National Museum, this bed-and-breakfast is just a three-minute walk to Wenceslas Square. The homey apartments and rooms are fully furnished down to the pots and pans. ✆ *Čelakovskeho sady 8 • Map G5 • 233 920118 • No air conditioning* • **K**

9 Hotel and Residence Standard

First-rate accommodation in a Jugendstil house along the Vltava. Nine double rooms and two suites. Guests have use of a private garage. Children under seven stay free. ✆ *Rašínovo nábřeží 38 • Map B6 • 224 916060 • www. standard.cz* • **KK**

10 Hotel Kliska

This guesthouse is situated in a quiet residential suburb of the city. The nearest metro station, Kobylisy (Line C), is a mere 5-minute walk away. From there, it is only five stops to the National Museum. ✆ *Veltěžská 26 • Map B5 • 233 920118 • www. hotelsprague.cz* • **KK**

Left **Hotel Residence Řetězová** Right **Palace Road Hotel**

⑩ Apartments

1 Apartment Lužická

This spacious, one-bedroom flat on a tree-lined Vinohrady street is tastefully appointed with simple furniture. The bright kitchen has all the utensils you need, a stocked refrigerator and a washing machine. ◈ *Lužická 14, Vinohrady • Map B6 • 251 512502, 775 588511 • www.apartments-in-prague.org • info@painfo.info • No air conditioning • K*

2 Hotel Residence Řetězová

A palace historically known as the House at the Three Golden Chains has been converted into nine spacious apartments. Each has vaulted ceilings, wooden floors and Italian baths. The Old Town location makes this the ideal base to explore the surrounding area. ◈ *Řetězová 9 • Map K5 • 222 221800 • www.residenceretezova.com • KKK*

3 Apartments Úvoz

Accommodation is in any of three converted art studios in a small Baroque-style house just below the Prague Castle. Ideal for those seeking privacy, tranquillity and a romantic setting. There are gorgeous views from the terrace on the roof. ◈ *Úvoz 24 • Map B2 • 233 920118 • www.hotelsprague.cz/uvoz • info@hotelsprague.cz • No air conditioning • KK*

4 Apartments Vlašská

These seven romantic apartments on a palace-lined Malá Strana street each have beautiful painted wooden beams, large windows, antique furniture and modern baths. ◈ *Vlašská 7–8 • Map B3 • 233 920118 • www.hotelsprague.cz/vlasska • Dis. access • No air conditioning • KK*

5 Alchymist Residence Nosticova

Tucked into a hidden corner of Malá Strana, the Nosticova is popular with film stars and other VIPs and celebrities. The apartments are decked out with such fine touches as antique clocks and crystal chandeliers. All this, and it's just a few minutes' walk from Charles Bridge. ◈ *Nosticova 1 • Map D3 • 257 312513 • www.nosticova.com • No air conditioning • KKKK*

6 Voyta Residence

Located just behind the National Theatre, these six apartments are spread across three different buildings. They are equipped with kitchens and en suite bathrooms with washing machines and are good value for money. ◈ *Vojtěšská 18 • Map B2 • 739 174685 • www.voytaresidence.cz • No air conditioning • KK*

7 Apartments U Císaře

This booking agency offers six apartments near metro and tram stop Jiřího z Poděbrad. Fully equipped kitchens and TVs help make guests comfortable. ◈ *Slezská 898/23, Vinohrady • Map B6 • 233 920118 • www.hotelsprague.cz/ucisare • No air conditioning • K*

8 Palace Road Hotel

These apartments and rooms make you feel like a pampered guest in a stately home. All of the bright rooms are furnished with period features and many have views over the city and Petřín park. ◈ *Nerudova 7 • Map C2 • 257 531941 • www.palaceroad.com • KK*

9 Residence Bene

Situated in the historical heart of Prague, the cosy apartments at Bene are a great alternative to a traditional hotel stay. The Palladium Shopping Centre is only a short distance away. ◈ *Dlouhá 48 • Map P3 • 222 313171 • www.goldencity.cz • KK*

10 Pension Klenor

Five kilometres (3 miles) from the city centre. There are 10 rooms, each with their own bath and satellite TV. Outdoor swimming pool. ◈ *Ve Studeném 6, Braník • 241 723240 • www.pensionklenor.cz • No air conditioning • K*

Many apartments have a minimum stay of at least three nights or one week – check when making a booking.

Above **Hotel Anna**

Price Categories

For a standard, double room per night (with breakfast if included), taxes and extra charges.

K	under Kč1,500
KK	Kč1,500–Kč3,000
KKK	Kč3,000–Kč4,500
KKKK	Kč4,500–Kč6,000
KKKKK	over Kč6,000

Hotels outside the City Centre

Hotel Diplomat

Near, but not within earshot of Ruzyně airport, the Diplomat has 398 rooms and all modern conveniences. Facilities include several restaurants, a business centre and an indoor go-cart track. Children under six stay free. Good access to the centre. ✆ *Evropská 15, Dejvice • Map A5 • 296 559111 • www.vi-hotels. com/en/diplomat • Dis. access* • **KKK**

Dorint Don Giovanni Prague

The Don Giovanni offers excellent value in the form of its 397 elegant rooms and 42 suites. Guests can take advantage of the spa-treatment facilities and baby-sitting service. The hotel is conveniently located near metro, bus and tram stops. ✆ *Vinohradská 157, Žižkov • Map B6 • 267 031111 • hotel-prag.dorint. com • Dis. access* • **KKK**

Hotel Le Palais

One of the finest examples of *belle epoque* architecture in Prague, this boutique hotel has plush rooms, attentive staff and a great wellness centre. The hotel also boasts a fine-dining restaurant on a hilltop, a luxury spa and a library. Wenceslas Square is just a 10-minute walk from here. ✆ *U Zvonařky 1, Vinohrady • Map B6 • 234 634111 • www. palaishotel.cz* • **KKKKK**

Hotel Belvedere

Located near Veletržní Palace, the Belvedere is a short walk to the Old Town or Prague Castle. Trams stop just outside. The rooms are very comfortable for the price. ✆ *Milady Horákové 19, Holešovice • Map B5 • 220 106111 • www.hotelbelvedere prague.cz • Dis. access* • **KK**

Louren Hotel

Built in 1889 as a block of flats, the Louren has had a rocky history, having been damaged in a US bombing raid in 1945 and nationalized after World War II. It is very luxurious, and the staff are delightful. ✆ *Slezská 55, Žižkov • Map B6 • 224 250025 • www.louren.cz* • **KK**

Hotel Anna

The Art Nouveau building in Vinohrady was built as a private residence at the end of the 19th century. The 26 rooms are decorated with engravings of historic Prague. From the top-floor suites, you can enjoy views of the castle and the Old Town. ✆ *Budečská 17 • Map B6 • 222 513111 • www. hotelanna.cz • Dis. access • No air conditioning* • **KK**

Hotel Vyšehrad

Behind the congress centre, close to the monuments of Vyšehrad, this hotel is fully up to date with satellite TV and Internet connections but holds on to its 19th-century charm. ✆ *Marie Cibulkové 29, Vyšehrad • Map B6 • 261 225592 • www.hotel-vysehrad.cz* • **KK**

Hotel Excellent

This small hotel lives up to its name if you don't mind being away from the crowd. Your hosts are happy to book flights, train tickets, seats at the opera or just show you around town. ✆ *Libeznická 164/19, Kobylisy • 284 687295 • www.hotel-excellent.cz • No air conditioning* • **KK**

Hotel Julián

Within walking distance of Malá Strana, the Julián is an Art Nouveau charmer. Guests will gush over the red-velvet lift and the fireside library. Some suites have a kitchen and there is a business centre and conference room. ✆ *Elišky Peškové 11, Smíchov • Map A6 • 257 311150 • www.julian.cz • Dis. access* • **KKK**

Akcent Hotel

This modern three-star hotel has splendid views of Prague from all 53 rooms. It is located on the seventh floor of a 1930s Functionalist-style office building. ✆ *Stroupežnického 1, Smíchov • Map A6 • 257 003494* • **KK**

Note: *Unless otherwise stated, all hotels accept credit cards, and have en-suite bathrooms and air conditioning.*

General Index

Acknowledgements

Main Contributor

Theodore Schwinke moved to the Czech Republic from the United States in 1996. A former editor of *The Prague Post*, his current projects include a children's book on the 16th-century Danish astronomer Tycho Brahe and a book on St Gorazd of Prague.

Produced by Sargasso Media Ltd, London

Project Editor
Zoë Ross

Art Editor
Philip Lord

Picture Research
Rhiannon Furbear, Helen Stallion

Proofreader
Stewart J Wild

Indexer
Hilary Bird

Editorial Assistance
Jakub Sverák

Main Photographer
Nigel Hudson

Additional Photography
Jiří Doležal, Jiří Kopřiva, Vladimìr Kozlik, František Přeučil, Milan Posselt, Rough Guides/Eddie Gerald, Rough Guides/Jon Cunningham/Helena Smith, Natascha Sturny,Stanislav Tereba, Peter Wilson

Illustrator
chrisorr.com

For Dorling Kindersley

Publishing Manager
Marisa Renzullo

Publisher
Douglas Amrine

Senior Cartographic Editor
Casper Morris

DTP
Jason Little

Production
Melanie Dowland

Picture Librarians
Hayley Smith, David Saldanha

Maps
Dominic Beddow, Simonetta Giori (Draughtsman Ltd)

Revisions Team
Emma Anacootee, Marta Bescos, Tessa Bindloss, Louise Cleghorn, Sherry Collins, Michelle Crane, Lydia Halliday, Scarlett O'Hara, Integrated Publishing Solutions, Lisa Jacobs, Bharti Karakoti, Sumita Khatwani, Tomáš Kleisner, Maite Lantaron, Tanya Mahendru, Marianne Petrou, Filip Polonsky, Beth Potter, Quadrum Solutions, Rada Radojicic, Ellen Root, Sands Publishing Solutions, Beverly Smart, Sadie Smith, Susana Smith, Leah Tether, Conrad van Dyk, Ajay Verma

Picture Credits

a-above; b-below/bottom; c-centre; f-far; l-left; r-right; t-top

Acknowledgements

The publishers would like to thank the following individuals, companies, and picture libraries for permission to reproduce their photographs:

AKG London: 11, 34tr, 35tl, 35 tr, 44tl, 44tc, 45tl, 45tr, 53t, Eric Lessing: 34b, 44b; ALAMY IMAGES: Adam Balatoni 129tr; Profimedia.CZ a.s./ Michaela Dusíková 126tl; Chris Fredriksson 50tr; AMBIENTE RESTAURANTS GROUP: 79tl, 96tr; AROMI: 123tl; ARTEL GLASS: 56tl; BAROCK: 103tl; BOHEMIA BAGEL: 88tl; CAFÉ SLAVIA: 60cla; THE CASTLE STEPS: 146tr; CHOCO STORY PRAHA: 51tl; CORBIS: 35bl, 44tr; LA CREPERIE: 122tl; CZECH TOURIST AUTHORITY: 1, 20–21, 70–71, 72tr, 73t, 90tl, 92t, 93r, 108–109, 118–19; CTK CZECH NEWS AGENCY: 4–5, 7t, 52tc, 52tr, 55br, 68tl, 68tr, 68c, 69bl, 69r, 76tr, 91t, 115b, 116, 117t, 122tr, 135tr; FORTEAN PICTURE LIBRARY: 52tl; RUUD JONKERS: 47r; KAPLAN PRODUCTIONS: 25, 35br, 45br, 52b; Courtesy of THE KOBAL COLLECTION:

Mandalay Entertainment 46b; Paramount Pictures 46tl; Portobello Pictures/Biograf Jan Sverak 46tr; Saul Zaenz Company 47tl; MECCA CLUB: 66tr; NATIONAL GALLERY OF PRAGUE: Paul Cézanne *House at Aix*, 1885-7 26c, Eugene Delacroix *Jaguar Attacking Horseman*, 27t, Paul Gauguin *Bonjour, Monsieur Gauguin*, 18, 26b, Vincent Van Gogh *Green Wheat*, 1889, 27b, Otto Gutfreund *Anxiety*, 1912–13, 7c, 27cr, Karlovy Lázné 66tl, 77tl; August Rodin *St John the Baptist*, 1878, 27c; NEBE COCKTAIL & MUSIC BAR: 111tr; PALÀC AKROPOLIS: 133tr; PRAGUE INFORMATION SERVICE: 94–95; PRAGUE INFORMATION SERVICE: RADISSON SAS ALCRON HOTEL: 62tl; THE RONALD GRANT ARCHIVE: Orion 46cl; ROPID: 137tl; STUDIO ŠPERK: 102tl; U PINKASŮ: 113tl; V RÀJI BOOKSHOP: 87TRI

All other images are © Dorling Kindersley. For further information see www.dkimages.com

Phrase Book

In an Emergency

Help!	**Pomoc!**	po-mots
Stop!	**Zastavte!**	zas-tav-te
Call a doctor!	**Zavolejte doktora!**	za-vo-ley-te dok-to-ra!
Call an ambulance!	**Zavolejte sanitku!**	za-vo-ley-te sa-nit-ku!
Call the police!	**Zavolejte policii!**	za-vo-ley-te poli-tsi-yi!
Call the fire brigade!	**Zavolejte hasiče**	za-vo-ley-te ha-si-che
Where is the telephone?	**Kde je telefón?**	gde ye te-le-fohn?
the nearest hospital?	**nejbližší nemocnice?**	ney-blizh-shee ne-mo-tsnyi-tse?

Communication Essentials

Yes/No	**Ano/Ne**	ano/ne
Please	**Prosím**	pro-seem
Thank you	**Děkuji vám**	dye-ku-ji vahm
Excuse me	**Prosím vás**	pro-seem vahs
Hello	**Dobrý den**	do-bree den
Goodbye	**Na shledanou**	na shle-da-nou
Good evening	**Dobrý večer**	do-bree ve-cher
morning	**ráno**	rah-no
afternoon	**odpoledne**	od-po-led-ne
evening	**večer**	ve-cher
yesterday	**včera**	vche-ra
today	**dnes**	dnes
tomorrow	**zítra**	zee-tra
here	**tady**	ta-di
there	**tam**	tam
What?	**Co?**	tso?
When?	**Kdy?**	gdi?
Why?	**Proč?**	proch?
Where?	**Kde?**	gde?

Useful Phrases

How are you?	**Jak se máte?**	yak se mah-te?
Very well, thank you.	**Velmi dobře, děkuji**	vel-mi do-brze dye-ku-yi
Pleased to meet you	**Těší mě**	tye-shee mnye
See you soon	**Uvidíme se brzy**	u-vi-dyee-me-se-brzy
That's fine	**To je v pořádku**	to ye vpo-rzhahdku
Where is/are…?	**Kde je/jsou …?**	gde ye/ysou …?
How long does it take to get to…?	**Jak dlouho trvá se dostat do…?**	yak dlou-ho ts tr-vah se dos-tat …?
How do I get to…?	**Jak se dostanu k …?**	yak se dos-ta-nuk …?
Do you speak English?	**Mluvíte anglicky?**	mlu-vee-te an-glits-ki?
I don't understand	**Nerozumím**	ne-ro-zu-meem
Could you speak more slowly?	**Mohl(a)* byste mluvit trochu pomaleji?**	mo-hl bys-te mlu-vit tro-khu..? po-ma-ley?
Pardon?	**Prosím?**	pro-seem?
I'm lost	**Ztratil(a)* jsem se**	stra-tyil (a) ysem se

Useful Words

big	**velký**	vel-kee
small	**malý**	ma-lee
hot	**horký**	hor-kee
cold	**studený**	stu-de-nee
good	**dobrý**	do-bree
bad	**špatný**	shpat-nee
well	**dobře**	dob-rzhe
open	**otevřeno**	o-tev-rzhe-no
closed	**zavřeno**	zav-rzhe-no
left	**do leva**	do-le-va
right	**do prava**	do-pra-va
straight on	**rovně**	rov-nye
near	**blízko**	blees-ko
far	**daleko**	da-le-ko
up	**nahoru**	na-ho-ru
down	**dolů**	do-loo
early	**brzy**	br-zi
late	**pozdě**	poz-dye
entrance	**vchod**	vkhod
exit	**východ**	vee-khod

toilets	**toalety**	to-a-le-ti
free, unoccupied	**volný**	vol-nee
free, no charge	**zdarma**	zdar-ma

Making a Telephone Call

I'd like to place a long-distance call	**Chtěl(a)* bych volat meziměstsky**	khtyel(a) bikh vo-lat me-zi mye-stski
I'd like to make a reverse-charge call	**Chtěl(a)* bych volat na účet volaného**	khtyel(a) bikh vo-lat na oo-chet vo-la-neh-ho
I'll try again later	**Zkusím to později**	sku-seem-to poz-dyey
Can I leave a message?	**Mohu nechat zprávu?**	mo-hu ne-khat sprah-vu?
Hold on	**Počkejte**	poch-key-te
local call	**místní hovor**	meest-nyee hovor

Sightseeing

art gallery	**galerie**	ga-le-ri-ye
bus stop	**autobusová zastávka**	au-to-bu-so-vah za-stah-vka
church	**kostel**	kos-tel
garden	**zahrada**	za-hra-da
library	**knihovna**	knyi-hov-na
museum	**muzeum**	mu-ze-um
railway station	**nádraží**	nah-dra-zhee
tourist information	**turistické informace**	tu-ris-tits-ke in-for-ma-tse
closed for the public holiday	**státní svátek**	staht-nyee svah-tek

Shopping

How much does this cost?	**Co to stojí?**	tso to sto-yee?
I would like …	**Chtěl(a)* bych …**	khtyel(a) bikh…
Do you have …?	**Máte …?**	maa-te …?
I'm just looking	**Jenom se dívám**	ye-nom se dyee-vahm
Do you take credit cards?	**Berete kreditní karty?**	be-re-te kre-dit nye kar-ti?
What time do you open/close?	**V kolik otevíráte/ zavíráte?**	v ko-lik o-te-vee-rah-te/ za-vee-rah-te?
this one	**tento**	ten-to
that one	**tamten**	tam-ten
expensive	**drahý**	d-ra-hee
cheap	**levný**	lev-nee
size	**velikost**	ve-li-kost
white	**bílý**	bee-lee
black	**černý**	cher-nee
red	**červený**	cher-ve-nee
yellow	**žlutý**	zhlu-tee
green	**zelený**	ze-le-nee
blue	**modrý**	mod-ree
brown	**hnědý**	hnye-dee

Types of Shop

antiques shop	**starožitnictví**	sta-ro-zhit-nyits-tvee
bank	**banka**	ban-ka
bakery	**pekárna**	pe-kahr-na
bookstore	**knihkupectví**	knih-ku-pets-tvee
butcher	**řeznictví**	rzhez-nyits-tvee
chemist (prescriptions etc)	**lékárna**	leh-kahr-na
chemist (toiletries etc)	**drogerie**	drog-erye
delicatessen	**lahůdky**	la-hood-ki
department store	**obchodní dům**	op-khod-nyee doom
grocery	**potraviny**	po-tra-vi-ni
glass	**sklo**	sklo
market	**trh**	trh
newsstand	**novinový stánek**	no-vi-no-vee stah-nek
post office	**pošta**	posh-ta
supermarket	**samoobsluha**	sa-mo-ob-slu-ha
tobacconist	**tabák**	ta-bahk
travel agency	**cestovní kancelář**	tses-tov-nyi kan-tse-laarzh

Staying in a Hotel

Do you have a vacant room?	**Máte volný pokoj?**	mah-te vol-nee po-koy?
double room	**dvoulůžkový pokoj**	dvou-loozh-ko-vee po-koy
with double bed	**s dvojitou postelí**	s dvoy-tou pos-te-lee
twin room	**pokoj s dvěma postelemi**	po-koy sdvye-ma pos-te-le-mi
room with a bath	**pokoj s koupelnou**	po-koj s kou-pel-nou
porter	**vrátný**	vraht-nee
I have a reservation	**Mám reservaci**	mahm rez-ervatsi

Eating Out

Have you got a table for …?	**Máte stůl pro …?**	mah-te stool pro …?
I'd like to reserve a table	**Chtěl(a)* bych rezervovat stůl**	khtyel(a) bikh re-zer-vo-vat stool
breakfast	**snídaně**	snyee-danye
lunch	**oběd**	ob-yed
dinner	**večeře**	ve-che-rzhe
The bill, please	**Prosím, účet**	pro-seem oo-chet
I am a vegetarian	**Jsem vegetarián(ka)***	ysem veghe-tariahn(ka)
waitress!	**slečno**	slech-no
waiter!	**pane vrchní!**	pane vrkh-nyee!
fixed-price menu	**standardní menu**	stan-dard-nyee menu
dish of the day	**nabídka dne**	na-beed-ka dne
starter	**předkrm**	przhed-krm
main course	**hlavní jídlo**	hlav-nyee yeed-lo
vegetables	**zelenina**	ze-le-nyi-na
dessert	**zákusek**	zah-kusek
cover charge	**poplatek**	pop-la-tek
wine list	**nápojový lístek**	nah-po-yo-vee lees-tek
rare (steak)	**krvavý**	kr-va-vee
medium	**středně udělaný**	strzhed-nye u-dye-la-nee
well done	**dobře udělaný**	dobrzhe-u-dye-la-nee
glass	**sklenice**	sklen-yitse
bottle	**láhev**	lah-hev
knife	**nůž**	noozh
fork	**vidlička**	vid-lich-ka
spoon	**lžíce**	lzhee-tse

Menu Decoder

biftek	bif-tek	steak
bílé víno	bee-leh vee-no	white wine
bramborové knedlíky	bram-bo-ro-veh kne-dleeki	potato dumplings
brambory	bram-bo-ri	potatoes
chléb	khlehb	bread
cibule	tsi-bu-le	onion
citrónový džus	tsi-tron-ove-ee dzhuus	lemon juice
cukr	tsukr	sugar
čaj	chay	tea
čerstvé ovoce	cher-stveh-o-vo-ce	fresh fruit
červené víno	cher-ven-eh vee-no	red wine
česnek	ches-nek	garlic
dort	dort	cake
fazole	fa-zo-le	beans
grilované	gril-ov-a-neh	grilled
houby	ho-bi	mushrooms
houska	hous-ka	roll
houskové knedlíky	ho-sko-veh kne-dleeki	bread dumplings
hovězí	hov-ye-zee	beef
hranolky	hra-nol-ki	chips
husa	hu-sa	goose
jablko	ya-bl-ko	apple
jahody	ya-ho-di	strawberries
jehněčí	ye-hnye-chee	lamb
kachna	kakh-na	duck
kapr	ka-pr	carp
káva	kah-va	coffee
kuře	ku-rzhe	chicken
kyselé zelí	kis-el-eh zel-ee	sauerkraut
maso	ma-so	meat
máslo	mah-slo	butter
minerálka	mi-ne-rahl-ka	mineral water
perlivá/	per-li-vah/	fizzy/
neperlivá	ne-per-li-vah	still
mléko	mleh-ko	milk
mořská jídla	morzh-skah yeed-la	seafood
ocet	o-tset	vinegar
okurka	o-kur-ka	cucumber
olej	oley	oil
párek	paa-rek	sausage
pečené	petsh-en-eh	baked
pečené	pech-en-eh	roast
pepř	peprzh	pepper
polévka	po-lehv-ka	soup
pomeranč	po-me-ranch	orange
pomerančový džus	po-me-ran-ch-o-vee dzhuus	orange juice
pivo	pi-vo	beer
rajské	rayskeh	tomato
ryba	ri-ba	fish
rýže	ree-zhe	rice
salát	sa-laat/sa-laht	salad
sůl	sool	salt
sýr	seer	cheese
šunka	shun-ka	ham
vařená/	va-rzhe-nah	cooked
uzená	u-zenah	smoked
telecí	te-le-tsee	veal
vajíčko	va-yeech-ko	egg
vařené	va-rzhe-neh	boiled
vepřovo-	vep-rzho-veh	pork
voda	vo-da	water
zelí	zel-ee	cabbage
zelenina	ze-le-nyi-na	vegetables
zmrzlina	zmrz-li-na	ice cream

Numbers

1	**jedna**	yed-na
2	**dvě**	dvye
3	**tř**	trzhi
4	**čtyři**	chti-rzhi
5	**pět**	pyet
6	**šest**	shest
7	**sedm**	sedm
8	**osm**	osm
9	**devět**	dev-yet
10	**deset**	de-set
11	**jedenáct**	ye-de-nahtst
12	**dvanáct**	dva-nahtst
13	**třináct**	trzhi-nahtst
14	**čtrnáct**	chtr-nahtst
15	**patnáct**	pat-nahtst
16	**šestnáct**	shest-nahtst
17	**sedmnáct**	sedm-nahtst
18	**osmnáct**	osm-nahtst
19	**devatenáct**	de-va-te-nahtst
20	**dvacet**	dva-tset
21	**dvacet jedna**	dva-tset yed-na
22	**dvacet dva**	dva-tset dva
30	**třicet**	trzhi-tset
40	**čtyřicet**	chti-rzhi-tset
50	**padesát**	pa-de-saht
60	**šedesát**	she-de-saht
70	**sedmdesát**	sedm-de-saht
80	**osmdesát**	osm-de-saht
90	**devadesát**	de-va-de-saht
100	**sto**	sto
1,000	**tisíc**	tyi-seets
2,000	**dva tisíce**	dva tyi-see-tse
5,000	**pět tisíc**	pyet tyi-seets
1,000,000	**milión**	mi-li-ohn

Time

one minute	**jedna minuta**	yed-na mi-nu-ta
one hour	**jedna hodina**	yed-na ho-dyi-na
half an hour	**půl hodiny**	pool ho-dyi-ni
day	**den**	den
week	**týden**	tee-den
Monday	**pondělí**	pon-dye-lee
Tuesday	**Úterý**	oo-te-ree
Wednesday	**středa**	strzhe-da
Thursday	**čtvrtek**	chtvr-tek
Friday	**pátek**	pah-tek
Saturday	**sobota**	so-bo-ta
Sunday	**neděle**	ned-yel-e